Cats, Clouds and Flatpacks

Cats, Clouds and Flatpacks

Magnie Shearer

The Shetland Times Ltd.
Lerwick
2009

Cats, Clouds and Flatpacks

ISBN 978 1 904746 48 5

First published by The Shetland Times Ltd., 2009.

Printed and published by
The Shetland Times Ltd.,
Gremista, Lerwick,
Shetland ZE1 0PX.

Contents

About the author

Magnie Shearer was born and brought up in Lerwick, Shetland, and for over 40 years has worked within the Isles. Initially starting out with the family firm of J&M Shearer Ltd, he continued in the fishing industry until retiring as a Director of LHD Ltd. He has also had a long association with the RNLI in Lerwick stretching back over 30 years. Always interested in the opportunity for a yarn or a story, he has finally put pen to paper. He is married with a wife and family, two grandsons, and a cat with attitude, and stays in Levenwick.

Five Airports

A fine sunny morning in Lerwick, and after having discussed our imminent departure with a grumpy Elwood the cat, and cautioned him on his recent skydiving attempts from the top of the shed into our tom-thumbs, we got the cases into the car and set off for Sumburgh.

Ten minutes later we were back again to collect the passports lying on the kitchen table, after the usual holiday conversation heading to the airport. *"Did you ...? No, I thought you ...!"* etc., etc.

Things began to look a trifle worrying as we sped past a bright and beautiful Quarff, up the hill and disappeared into a wall of grey fog and rain. *"Oh, it'll be clearer when we get farther south ..."*

Hah! The only thing clearer as we crested the brow of the hill down into Sumburgh was the fact that even a pin would have difficulty getting through all the enveloping mugginess that surrounded us.

Still, we found a parking place in the original slots right next to the airport terminal – I nearly took a photo of this rare phenomena as

1

normally we end up nearer the lighthouse – and felt things were maybe looking up. We duly joined the queue for the check-in to be greeted by those who had already endured this process with their cheery smiles and friendly words, *"Flights all delayed, no word of anything flying so far, and the boat's full up with no berths or reclining seats either!"*

Magic, and thought better of suggesting a night lying on the floor onboard the *Hrossey*, at this moment in time, as they say. We checked in and a very pleasant lass took our cases and gave us boarding passes, which we both knew were about as much use as a chocolate fireguard, and exchanged pleasantries about our hopes and aspirations of flying to Glasgow.

Relieved of our two trolley cases, and grasping our trusty backpack and handbag respectively we settled down in the chairs opposite the television screens, had a quick look around the terminal to see anybody I recognised, and divided them into two distinct groups: the ones you are happy to chat to who you know will go away and leave you in peace to worry yourself sick about the prospect of flying in mist; and those who latch onto you like a dog in heat and spend a while giving you snippets of terrifying information such as *"It must be hellish flying in conditions like this, they only have about 20-30 seconds to make a decision whether to land or abort."*

At this point you have now worked out an escape route via the toilets, by standing on the cistern and climbing out the window – only to discover on your first attempt that the men's toilets are entirely windowless.

You wash your hands three times and dry them four times, as delaying tactics, and finally emerge like a startled rabbit into the bright lights of the terminal. You cautiously make your way back to your seat by a circuitous route, only to be met by friends who know you too well and say, *"Whatever happened to you, you were ages in there, you didn't splash the front of your trousers again did you?"*

This little gem relates to the fact that I rather like to wear my khaki chinos when going off on 'holiday', as I like to think we're heading for the sun, and it sort of psychologically prepares me for the trip ahead. However ... I am not the best at handling new fangled taps in washrooms, and her little reference to the trousers concerns a certain occasion just before a previous flight where I nipped off into the toilet, did the business and, standing in front of the sink, pushed the 'automatic' tap downwards as instructed. In a second a torrent of hot water gushed out of the tap, circled the basin and shot out directly covering my nether regions leaving a large wet stain, only too evident on my nice lightly coloured chinos! At the same time, the Tannoy belted out a warning that gate such and such was closing for flight BA whatever, and after desperately trying to wipe the water off the front of my trousers, I decided cleverly to use the hand drier.

Now, as you may know, this is located about four feet off the floor, so I was in quite a tricky position with my crotch as high as I could get it near the chrome direction vent, my leg resting on the sink unit, like a dog having a pee against a wall ... when in comes a pilot. "Hi," says I, in a nonchalant sort of way, as you would do standing drying your crotch in an airport washroom, and smiled stupidly. He just glanced at me, my precarious position, my trousers, and I could see him put two and two together – and make three – not, I fear, the true answer to my need for the use of the hand-dryer!

So, so ... onwards and upwards, we sat and read books, watched the arrivals/departures screens, television channels and then every now and then, a smiley, smarmy TV weather presenter would pop-up on the screen to tell us we were soooo lucky with the weather and wasn't this heat wave just marvellous, " ... *as the whole of the country is basking in sunshine today.*" Tosser.

Six hours into the event, and various announcements none of which filled me with confidence, they finally told us we could collect vouchers for food and refreshments from the check-in desk. I was second in the queue, not wanting to look too desperate, and we made our way to the airport shop and exchanged them for a varied selection of food. Mmmm.

Then it was back to the desk to join the rest of the happy band of travellers who were being given a variety of choices, not many of which seemed to involve onward travel of any sort. Some folks in the queue were lamenting the fact that their flight to Florida was at 6 o'clock the next morning and they just didn't know how they were going to catch it. Now I'm not being rude here, but just how many cans short of a carry out are these numpties? Who in their right minds would arrange to fly out of Shetland less than a day before an international flight half across the world – here we were two days before the Glasgow premiere of 'Garfield the Movie 2' – and I was moderately distressed that I might not make it. These folks hadn't a hope of catching their planned flight to the old U S of A.

Once again a very pleasant lass re-booked us, on the Edinburgh flight at 0730 the next morning there being no seats available on the Glasgow flight. We were looking forward to getting up again at 0530 to shave the cat, wash the cornflakes and other such things you do at this ungodly hour of the morning when your brain is still on sleep mode.

The following day dawned bright and breezy, things were looking good. I kissed Elwood goodbye again and we discussed briefly his latest skydiving efforts onto our next-door neighbours' head. This we agreed was not a 'good idea', but I fear he took little heed as I could see the glint in his eye as I left.

The sun was still shining as we climbed out of Lerwick and motored along the road, humming a happy little tune. Suddenly, Waoomph ... Gulberwick was covered in the stuff, miles and miles of thick grey cloud, mist, fog, call it what you want. But by Quarff it was bright again. Hooray. All the way to Channerwick, then straight into it again ... all the way to Sumburgh. Superb.

Check in at 0630, after joining a queue that stretched right out the door, and exchanging various degrees of deprivation with other frequent flyers. At the desk, a very agreeable fellow with a slightly strained smile told me in a low voice that he didn't think there was a cat's chance in hell of us getting out of here till the following afternoon at best, as he handed me our boarding cards for the Edinburgh flight. We thanked him, for what I'm not sure, and took up position in the TV seats again.

Six hours later they cancelled the flights and I had had three escape attempts aborted by the security staff, who now had me on a 'red alert', as various guys who worked there would pass by and say things like: "How many coffees today then, Magnie?" "You want to watch your caffeine intake, it plays havoc with your hormones."

I could do with some HRT I'm telling you, this flying business is way over-rated if you ask me.

Back to the check-in desk and some 'buddy-buddy' stuff with the staff just so they remember I'm still here, and another re-booking session whereby we are back on the Glasgow flight, this time for the next day. This is our last attempt; otherwise it's just not worth going as we will shortly be getting there a few hours after we should be on the return flight. More 'buddy-buddy' stuff and an agreement that though we are No's 16 and 17 on the standby list they will see if they can get us on any flight that should fly out of Shetland to anywhere, anytime, today. Hospital cases etc., get priority apparently which is perfectly acceptable, and I consider phoning Cornhill to see if they have any spare places, but others feel that this is possibly a bit too extreme. Not in my eyes, as I start swinging from the stair-rails in an attempt to fill in an hour or so. Security talks me down eventually.

Elvis has not left the building, and nor have we. It pays off. The nice girl at the check-in desk summons me to the counter and tells me they are booking us on the Inverness flight. Now, when I said anywhere I was thinking Aberdeen, Edinburgh, Glasgow, but what the hell, it's Scotland, the mainland, the middle of teuchter country – we'll go. Frantic re-checking in. No, nobody has given me anything to take onboard, no I don't have any pointy things on my person, yes I know the photo on the passport looks like a monkey on speed, but that's me and sad as it may seem that's what I look like. Just give me the boarding passes. Ok, we're off.

No time to worry. Through the x-ray machine, switch off mobile phone, go to the toilet in the departure lounge – why, oh why, so many coffees. Stand four feet away from the sink, wash my hands and most of the floor – Hah! – missed me! Dry them in my shirt and, Oh God, the door's locked. No amount of pulling will move it. I'm trapped. I'm going to miss my flight, the first to get out of here in three days. Dear Lord, what next. Uh-Huh ... it opens out, you push it. Numpty. Again. Right we're in, seats 2C and 2D, bang in the front, right opposite the entrance door, the flight attendant's jump seat, and can see directly into the cockpit. Not my favourite, but there's masses of legroom as no seats in front. That'll do nicely. Watch as the attendant hauls the door shut, pulls a lever here and there, and I want to get up and just check she's done it right, but my wife thinks I should just sit still and belt up. Possibly in more ways than one. The attendant gets into her jump seat and puts on a full harness, not the thing we strap around our middles, but the bees-knees, the full monty, the works. Ok, so if in the event we come to a sudden stop she's going to be ok, while the plane is full of the top halves of passengers bouncing around the seats. Hmmm.

The pilot comes on and tells us his name. Charlie Hemple-Smith, or some such thing, has that half-American drawl that is intended to make you relax. Ok folks, it's going to be fine, we're just off for a stroll in the woods etc. *"We should be flying at ... Oh, I dunno ... 10,000 ft ... or so. The weather at Kirkwall is unfortunately not looking good at the moment, but we will go and have a look."*

Kirkwall ...? Kirkwall ...? I thought we were going to Inverness? Oh yea, right, we have to go via Kirkwall, if we get there.

We do. Charlie lands it like a bouncing bomb on the runway and after a couple of hops and skips we're there. The co-pilot comes out of the cockpit, and she's a tall, blonde Jessica Simpson look-a-like. I can see why Charlie made such a tots of landing the thing. His mind was not on his instruments.

Ten minutes and we're off again, heading deep into hoochty choochty territory. Inverness looms up in around 25 minutes, and after a free double vodka and coke life is beginning to look a bit brighter. We land without the kangaroo hops, and I'm guessing Jessica was at the wheel this time. No problem. Taxi into Inverness. Splendid feed in the Pizza Express, right next door to the station, complete with live jazz music and a feisty little red wine.

Onto the Scotrail 2013 train to Glasgow Queen Street via Perth and a few shinty towns besides. We clamber aboard, get our cases stowed, settle down and nod pleasantly to a group of four Americans from the *'Texas Large Facial Hair Association'* sitting next to us, and watch as Kingussie, Newtonmore, and Pitlochry shoot past the windows.

The air conditioning was on full blast as the lucky sods had been enduring the northern end of the 'heat wave that was sweeping the country', but as the night darkened and the sun disappeared behind the mountains it was feeling distinctly chilly. My wife snuggled up to me and borrowed my jacket, together with her jacket and fleece, and was soon nodding off; while I sat and listened to the Yanks reminisce.

"Heh, Buck, d'ya see that deer out there?"

Buck? Yes, that was our hero's name – a dead ringer for Craig Stadler the golfer, who in turn resembles a large walrus. You get the picture.

"Yea, Ah saw him – red or dead – them deers look good."

There then followed a discussion on guns and other shooty things. I suppose in America every day is the same weather wise, so they talk about guns.

"Ah remember the time ma aunt was having big problems with her banshees, and the old cockerel was servicing them all. Gee, she was ending up with chickens all o'er the place and half of them was roosters too.

"She asked me to come and try and cull a few of them for her. So I brought out ma 56 Magnum, and blasted them outa da state. Geez it was like shootin pillows – god damn feathers everywhere!"

After an hour or so they fell asleep, and snored away happily as more Highland place names sped past. I amused myself by conjuring up firms of solicitors out of the villages we trundled through. Messrs Dunkeld Birnam & Dalwhinnie – "Just take a seat sir, Mr Birnam will see you shortly".

Another happy moment is spent watching people attempt to enter the Tardis Machine that doubles as a Scotrail toilet compartment. These round obtrusions in the middle of a train are semi-automatic in that the doors are operated by an air system which only works by pushing a button located low down on the far side. Numerous circumnavigations are done by the various people in ever increasing discomfort, until they finally find the red button and magically the door opens and in they go, with the door closing quietly behind them. After a few minutes the door opens and the said occupant shoots out of the unit like a missile and stands back examining the creature which has very nearly swallowed them whole. Eventually they leave and we sit and await the approach of another unsuspecting customer.

Just at this point the leading walrus stirs and wakens, emits a loud snort, and looks at me, looks out the window, looks directly down the train carriage then turns to his fellow associates and says, *"Gee, where the hell are we?"*

"We're in Scautlaand, Hank – same place we've been for the last three weeks."

"Oh yea, gee this train is slow."

Hmmm.

You can see where they got G. W. Bush from now.

The country's full of them.

Scary.

At around 2200 we arrive in Perth and a midget joins the train, dressed in Scotrail uniform with around 15 sets of keys hanging from every pocket, lapel, button, belt, he's wearing. Up to now each station has been announced with clear and precise detail. But things are set to change. We trundle on and eventually at 2336 we arrive at *"Wean Shite Stitchin"* and are advised by the midget that *"Aw pissin jars hiv tae gaet aff here, and tae min thae tak aw yir kisses an at."*

Superb. We're in Glasgow and a two minute ride in a black cab driven by Darth Vader and we're at The Express by Holiday Inn. The Cowcaddens fire engines and ambulance speed past in convoy with a welcoming wail of their sirens. We've arrived at last. Garfield here we come.

Five Airports – The Return

We had a splendid two days in Glasgow, met up with my cousin, her husband and their two boys. Together with her sister and my aunt and uncle we spoke rubbish, had a ball with the boys and generally enjoyed ourselves immensely. We also managed to have meatballs at IKEA, Italian, Thai and Spanish meals, various assorted beers in various licensed premises, and do a bit of shopping.

The weekend we happened to choose coincided with the Glasgow Trades Fairs Holiday Fortnight or some such title, and so the streets were busy. Very busy. The weather was excellent, high 20s, sunny and a light wind. As a result I gave up on seeing the premiere of *Garfield*, too many neds and not enough baby boomers, and the queues at the Kelvingrove Museum were enormous. They will both keep for another day.

We managed to shop well again, and I sauntered and soaked up a bit of the Buchanan Street atmosphere. Buskers, Break Dancers, Balloon Sellers, Bobby Dazzlers and a fair collection of out and out

Bampots. All good fun and what makes Glasgow a great city to visit. The Next '50% Sale' opened the Saturday we were there, and all the women folk advised that they would not be going near the place as it was absolute bedlam. Music to my ears. I ventured in for a look around mid morning, just to see what this was all about.

Now, if you've ever been into Next on a normal day it's busy, but very well organised, everything is in its place, all neatly stacked, labelled, priced and displayed. On Sale Day things are a bit different. The place looked like a bomb had hit it. There were clothes strewn everywhere, security men in droves, shoes stacked 12 pairs high on shelves, with cable ties securing the left and right. I was idly wandering past this collection of mayhem when a loud voice behind me says, *"Haw Big Yin, is you'se buying or sniffing, byraway!"*

I turned round and this small runt of a guy dressed in half a purple shell-suit and an Argentinian football shirt was standing right behind me. *"Na, in you go pal,"* says I, slipping into the vernacular.

"Cheers Mac," he says, nips in past me, grabs a pair of Adidas trainers, *"Ya beauty!"*, and makes off for the checkout. Brilliant. Glasgow. City of Culture.

Sunday dawned bright and sunny, the perfect day for flying. We climbed into a yellow Glasgow taxicab and had a fine run out to the airport as the driver regaled us with tales of his mother, brother, sister-in-law and third cousin, all who appeared to have played for Partick Thistle at some time.

The airlines have this great system now whereby you shove your credit card into their e-ticket machine and, after pushing a few screen symbols, it spews out your boarding passes. Away we go and off to the 'Fast Bag Drop' – except it isn't now. Everybody is using the e-ticket machine, or if not then two Smile School graduates are steering them into it, and so we all now join a queue the same length as the former check-in queue to drop our bags – fast.

Another very fine lass on the desk tells us there are no problems with our flight, and wishes us a safe journey and hopes we will fly with them again.

She's lying through her teeth of course; thick mist at Sumburgh, the Glasgow flight has never left Shetland. It has never got in from Edinburgh. It has never got back from Shetland the night before. There aren't enough Saab 340s. The 0730 from Shetland to Edinburgh becomes the 0940 from Edinburgh to Shetland, which becomes the 1140 from Shetland to Glasgow, which becomes the 1330 from Glasgow to Shetland, which becomes the 1530 from Shetland to Edinburgh, which becomes the 1740 back to Shetland, which becomes the 0730 ...

We wander around Glasgow airport and I find a large TV screen that isn't displaying a weather forecast and watch the final round of the Open Golf. Tigger appears to be doing well. Bouncy, pouncy, flouncy ... *"It's another beautiful day here, and I'm sure like the rest of the country you're all enjoying this glorious weather ..."* Sod off. Again.

We go through departures and sit down. Recognise various fellow travellers all kidding themselves we'll soon be boarding the flight. Crackle, crackle and in among the clicks and whistles we're told our flight has been cancelled. Back to Ticket Information Desk. No seats available on Glasgow flights for Monday. Edinburgh 0940 or 1740. Go for 0940, I'm supposed to be back at work Monday morning.

Number one bus Glasgow Airport to Glasgow Buchanan Street. The driver wants to be Lewis Hamilton. We bounce and crash our way through the traffic, but he has a poor day. He doesn't hit anyone. Lug our cases off the bus and off into the terminal. Two tickets Glasgow Buchanan Street-Edinburgh St Andrews Square. Citylink. Lug our cases onboard and away we go. Very fine bus. Onboard toilet locked though. Hmmm. Get off at Princes Street. Lug our cases along the road and down Waverley Bridge to the Airport Express bus. Lug our cases onboard and head off to Edinburgh Airport. The driver is another budding Formula 1 expert. We rattle and swing our way through the city, past the Zoo, where I think the conductor has just escaped from, and arrive at Edinburgh Airport. Lug our cases off the bus and trundle off to the courtesy bus stop for the airport hotel. Lug our cases onboard his minibus and set off. We slide around the seats as he tackles the roundabouts with gay abandon, and I hang onto the metal uprights like some demented pole dancer.

We check into the hotel. Last room available. Twin room. Hope the airport noise doesn't disturb you sir. No, no. Just sheer envy at the lucky so and so's who are actually flying off somewhere. Pint of Worthington's, an excellent feed, meet up with more relations, catch up, speak rubbish and generally have a ball.

Monday dawns bright and beautiful. The waiters in the restaurant for breakfast are all ex-KGB or Stasis or similar. Can't understand a word he's saying and she's not much better. Just agree and wait excitedly to see what they bring us. A large brown offering resembling a dog poo arrives on a plate and is set down with a flourish and a few more words of East European origin. I think it's a croissant, so cover it liberally with marmalade and drink my coffee. He then arrives with my wife's offering, 12 slices of brown toast. Think maybe we have a communication problem here, but nod happily and he does the same. We eat all we need and rise from the table. He nods, we nod, she nods, we nod, he nods, we nod, she – for goodness sake get out of here.

A friendly lass at the check-in tells us she has no record of us, our flight, our aircraft, our island. After a few phone calls, she smiles and tells us everything is ok, she's found us. We get our boarding passes 10C and 10D. Not the 7C and 7D I was hoping for, the emergency seats, the ones with lots of legroom. Never mind, we're maybe going to get home. The flight has left Shetland an hour late admittedly but is on its way. Hooray.

We climb onboard and into an oven. It must be 30-40 degrees in here, the sun is beating down on the plane and until they shut the doors no air conditioning can work. There's always some doom-laden merchant sitting behind you who talks loudly and incessantly. *"Folk can die in this heat you know. They don't even transport cattle like this. I can't think they will fly with all these passengers onboard, the plane must be overloaded … "*

Charlie Hemple-Smith's cousin is flying the plane. He's even more laid back. *"Oh … Hello … This is your Captain speaking … …*

Ahmmm mumble, mumble ... crackle ... crackle ... 19,000 ft ... Louise is your flight attendant ... comfort ... tea and coffee ... pay particular attention ... ... click."

We're off, the cooling kicks in, the sun's shining, the clouds are lovely and white, Louise is struggling up the passage with a trolley with a mind of its own. We balance piping hot coffee, plastic bags sealed for eternity containing the vital sugar, a wooden stick, more plastic bags sealed for eternity with crumbly biscuits, napkins. And of course the infamous mini milk cartons. Light coloured chinos, mini milk cartons – a recipe for disaster.

My wife takes over very quickly, just as I was about to burst the whole contents over the both of us. She neatly opens a corner, peels back the lid and empties it into my coffee cup, expertly. I lift the coffee cup and knock my hand against the folded down tray which is squashing me into the seat.

It takes only 10 minutes to clean the seats, me, and the guy in front's head with the fourteen napkins kindly supplied by Louise. I decline her offer of another cup. Well, actually, my fellow traveller declined her offer, rather too quickly I thought.

Charlie's cousin tells us all to look out the window and see Fair Isle. Which we do, and Louise tells us it's ten minutes to landing, and twenty minutes later we bounce onto the runway having come in kamikaze style over the lighthouse.

After five airports, four buses, three taxis, two planes and a train, we're home again. Flying, it's the only way to travel.

The Day We Moved

According to psychiatrists and others who make a living out of studying human nature, moving home is the third most traumatic experience in life after bereavement and divorce. That may be a bit over dramatic, but it certainly ranks up there in the *"Where the Hell's the Aspirin"* scale of things pretty highly.

It's not that we hadn't planned for it, or that it suddenly came out of the blue, in fact we had gone about it all in a remarkably civilised manner and the last night in the old house took on an air of calm resignation. All was already packed up and moved to the new house, the last bits and pieces were all in a box to take with us and we were looking forward to moving in the following day.

I had spent a productive afternoon and evening clearing out the last of the rubbish from the garage and had filled a Transit van with a huge assortment of useless items I had 'saved' over the years. Things like tins of paint long since solidified, offcuts of wood that were never going to be used again except for firewood, jam jars of now rusty nails of various sizes welded together, bolts of wallpaper faded into oblivion, old rabbit hutches with doors missing, a set of angel's wings from Halloween, the bottom half of a giraffe suit, old car tyres, bits of bicycle chain, half a broken tea set, pieces of a knitting machine, a long since punctured blow up globe of the world ... the list was endless, and Steptoe and Son were mere amateurs compared to my ability to accumulate junk – "it will always come in handy some day".

That day was always going to be the day after tomorrow, and suddenly, inexplicably, I would find a need for a set of angel's wings or a punctured globe. Tonight, however, they were destined for the rubbish dump at the Rova Head. So it was that I had closed up the van with great difficulty, virtually leaning with all my weight on the two back doors until finally succeeding in jamming them shut. Suitably sustained after a cuppa tea and a digestive, I ventured out to the van about midnight and was just checking it was all secure when I heard a rustle behind me and a voice said, *"Excuse me, is this your dog?"*

I looked around and there, standing in the dark, was an unknown woman leading a Hush Puppy dog on a bit of string. This low slung Basset Hound gave me a look and I could swear he rolled his eyes at me as I sized up the situation.

"No," says I, *"our dog's a Jack Russell and he's fast asleep upstairs in the house."*

"Oh, well I don't know what I'm going to do," she replied. *"This thing has been sitting howling its head off outside our window all night."*

"Well, maybe it's from the next road," I ventured, though I did think to myself I hadn't seen Boris, as I decided to call him, anywhere near here.

"I can't go on like this," she says, *"I'm getting no sleep at all, and he won't go away."*

I gave old Boris another look, and he just shrugged, rolled his eyes again and gave a head to tail wiggle. He knew where he stayed but wasn't letting on; he was obviously having a bit of fun singing his heart out on this woman's doorstep. It was at this point I noticed that the woman was pregnant, very pregnant, as in possibly 10 or 11 months pregnant and so, as I didn't want to excite her too much and start an explosion of sorts, I was considering calmly suggesting that we maybe should all just go home and go to bed now.

However, she had other ideas.

"Can you take me to the Police Station and I can hand this stupid dog into them to look after and then I'll get some sleep?"

Not wanting to exacerbate the situation anymore I agreed, and Boris gave me a hard look and I figured maybe we would have trouble with him later.

So, I opened the passenger door of the Transit van and in a very quick movement for what had seemed a slow old dog, Boris was in and took up his position centre stage in the middle of the three seats in the van. The woman, meantime, was struggling a bit as she was determined not to let go of the bit of string attached to Boris, and in the end I had to assist her vertically upwards and into the side seat of the van. A delicate task at the best of times but with a pregnant woman you don't know, in an overly sensitive state, tied to a huffy dog, it made finding the correct handholds all the more complicated. However, all went well with no mishaps and I came round and got in the driver's seat. We then set off for the Police Station. Expectant Mum, Boris and Me.

On arriving at the end of the road, where it joins the main South Road, we duly stopped at the junction and as I checked for vehicles I was aware that at my side Boris was doing a very good impression of the Green Cross Code. He sat upright and leaned forward, swung his head left, right and left again, catching me a quick slap around the face with his long heavy ears, then looked up at me, nodded and sat back again. All was clear, we could go. For goodness sake, what am I doing here?

The same thing happened at every junction until we reached the Police Station. At this point I really wasn't keen to become involved in a lost dogs scenario so suggested that I would drive up to the station, slip the dog and the expectant lady off, then turn the van around. This was met with approval and off they both went. Boris, I must say, had a sort of jaunty swagger to him as he loped off up to the station door, and I suspect he may have been a regular client. Some time later, formalities completed, she emerged alone, with Boris presumably in some cell somewhere awaiting collection, and the return journey ensued.

This was all eating into my 'Rova Head' disposal plan but, however, we finally turned back in the road and headed towards the house, and at this point she looked across at me and said, *"I just don't know what Donald will make of all this!"*

"Donald? ... Who's Donald?" I asked, mildly interested in this sudden revelation, as up to this point I had assumed she was home alone and struggling with Boris all on her own.

"Donald? ... Well Donald's my husband," she answered.

"I see ... Hmmm ... And where is Donald at the moment?" I enquired.

"Oh, Donald's asleep in his bed," she replied.

"Asleep in his bed ... Ok, he couldn't take you and the dog to the station then?"

"Oh no ... I didn't want to disturb him ..."

"Well ... Hellooooo ...!" At this point in my mind's eye I could see the word 'Plonker' in large letters across my forehead and began to think ... You great big numpty, Shearer!

Still, I dropped her off at the house and saw her safely in the door before revving up the engine and heading off down the driveway. Not much point really, as Boris hadn't wakened Donald there was probably no way I was going to either. Never mind, my good deed for the day done, I set off to the Rova Head with my head held high. On arrival there it was now well past midnight and the lights were all off, I parked the van, opened the doors and couldn't see a bloody thing. There was no way I could find anything in the total darkness and after a few attempts to haul bits out I gave up, closed up the van doors and headed home again!

The next morning I was up early and headed off to the dump and managed to get all the rubbish out and into the skips. Magic, and as I drove home I passed a guy walking a Basset Hound along the main road. I looked hard at the dog, and I could have sworn he nodded and gave me a wink, but then again …

The Wrong Trousers

This all took place when I was in the hospital after a heart attack a few years ago. I've had the treadmill ECG test a number of times now and I was a smarter bunny on the next occasions having already been through the mill, so to speak. As happens when you're admitted to the hospital in an emergency, you thank God for all the times your Mam told you to remember and wear clean underwear every day, *"Because you never know when you might be knocked down and taken to the hospital"* – embarrassment being the main thing in life in the fifties – death or injury were just secondary!

So, though I had on clean underwear and the rest, I don't generally sleep in pyjamas, just boxers and the like. Which was fine, but the powers that be decided I would have to undergo this treadmill test to see if the heart was damaged or still working etc. So we were hurled down to the ECG room in a wheelchair, with one of those back-to-front gowns resembling a curtain with the tie-backs at the rear and obviously introduced by some NHS guy with a kinky sense of humour They make you feel more naked than naked. They had also decided that I would need to change into the hospital pyjamas and had whipped off my boxers and I was all alone with nothing but this hospital gown in their place.

We duly arrived at the treatment room and there on the bench was their pride and joy in the jim-jams department – faded red and white striped hospital issue men's pyjama trousers, the elastic of which had lost its elasticity many moons ago. Super – I got behind this modesty screen as they called it, and I waffled about trying to get into these things, and discovered they must be about a waist size 50, and I'm a 36. Uh Huh ... We have a small problem here!

I did mention this on emerging from behind the screen, but was brushed aside as this guy attacked me with sandpaper *("to make sure the electrodes get a good grip")*. For the love of God – by the time he was finished I looked like some starling with the measles – red marks all over where he'd scrubbed away. Anyway, he then connected up the wires and so on, and fitted the blood pressure cuff on the other arm and trailed cables from there to another machine, and we were ready for the off. I'm now standing gripping the tops of the pyjama trousers with one hand and trying to keep my balance on the treadmill as he started the thing up.

These two nurses and a doctor were now poised next to me to study the machines' readings, and presumably give the kiss of life if I popped over mid-tread.

"You'll have to hold on, Mr Shearer," she says, *"as the angle and slope of the treadmill changes and the speed increases."*

Angle? Slope? Speed? Nobody told me about trying to battle uphill as well as straight ahead – I could see we were in for a bit of sport. Right enough, the blessed thing started to get faster and faster, and tilted slowly upwards – I swandered around on it and the doctor shouts ... *"Hold on, Mr Shearer, or you'll fall."* Hold on, I *am* holding on – to the tops of my pyjamas, but I can see he has a point as I just about go arse over tip and disappear out the back end of the machine. I grip the rails, and try to hold on to the trousers with the arm with the

BP cuff attached, but the cables and tubes get in a right jumble, and I have to try and swap hands.

Now, if you've ever slipped on an icy patch on the pavement, but just managed to keep your balance, what do you do? Yea, that's right, you look down or behind you at the spot as, of course, it's the entire ground's fault. Well, the same applies to the treadmill, as when I wavered about on the belt I looked down, and that was a mistake – as I kind of lurched into the side and had to grip the rails with both hands – and, oh boy ... that was when things started to go seriously wrong.

On gripping with both hands I had to forgo any attempt to keep the trousers up. I could feel them starting to slip and said to the guy to slow the thing down.

"Oh, are you not feeling too well, Mr Shearer?" he says (making no attempt to slow it down at all I might add).

"No, no," says I, "it's the trousers, they're going to fall down."

"Whose trousers?" he says, looking around at the doctor and the nurses!

"My ones!" says I, but fate had taken hold and they were by now slipping ever so slowly earthwards.

"Oh, I don't think so," he says, as they fell to a heap around my ankles.

Now I'm doubly in trouble as I can hardly keep my feet on the blasted treadmill anyway, and I've now got a pair of oversized pyjamas wittered about my ankles, and I have to try and keep up a merry little canter just to stay upright!

Jeez – what a carry on. I am also trying to hide my embarrassment, hold on to the rails, haul up the trousers, and half run/jog/dance all at the same time – it's no wonder the BP readings were bouncing out the top!

In my attempts to keep walking, one leg of the pyjamas came away from my foot and in seconds the second leg did the same, and in a flash – no pun intended – I saw them shoot past me and out the back of the machine onto the floor, where I couldn't reach them! Dear God – here I am 'jogging' as fast as I can to stay upright, starkers on a treadmill, with a male doctor, a technician and two female nurses in attendance.

As they say, when you're five nothing embarrasses you, 15 to 25 everything embarrasses you, and over 55 nothing embarrasses you again – so I just stuck to the latter and thankfully they got the machine stopped and I could retrieve the pyjama trousers and come to some sense of decorum!

They made me lie down after all that – I think just so they could have a rest from giggling and laughing – nothing to do with me being knackered (in more ways than one). The end result was I had to do it all again, so you know what they did – they stuck the pyjama trousers to my stomach with strips of surgical tape! The tossers!

Still, it held, and they got their readings and a fair bit of my stomach hair as well, as souvenirs. I survived to tell the tale, and sometime I'll maybe give you an account of another exciting day in the hospital, when I had a procedure called a sigmoidoscopy, the younger brother of the full monty, the colonoscopy. Suffice to say it involved a lot of rubber tubing and you get to know how Sooty feels ... but we really don't want to go there.

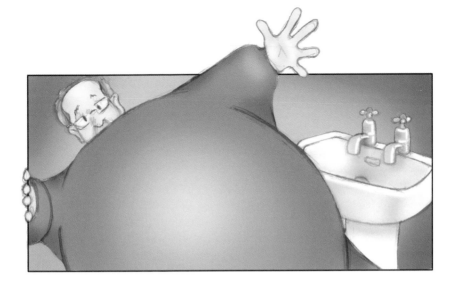

Mad as a Bag of Frogs

Friday dawned bright and sunny and all seemed well with the world until, about five minutes into the shower, I remembered that in a weak moment I had promised that I would take the Hippo suit north with me to Busta for the retirement party that night.

Why, oh why, do I always find myself in these situations? One day, some day, I WILL say no to folks! But, of course, secretly I kind of enjoy the nonsense and the fun, so God forbid the day I take life too seriously.

So, quarter to seven at night and I'm off in the car, Hippo in the boot, to pick up an assortment of various medical people and a chocolate cake, and journey north to Busta House. I have visions of a yowe running across the road, me having to brake quickly, and someone in the back seat being violently propelled headfirst into the bowels of the chocolate cake!

However, we arrived safely and all the introductions were made. *"Oh, this is Magnie ... have you not met him?"*

Magic ... here's me among a few well known faces, but also an array of medics I've never seen before and I'm about to burst into their lives dressed in an inflatable Hippo suit. Hmmmm ... Why, oh why ...

After a splendid meal and having been placed at the long table of 16 nurses, where the conversation was varied and interesting to say the least, with topics ranging from Rayburns, through bolero tops and their fastening arrangements, to Chinese herbal remedies for period pains (where I finally had to give in and admit I had no real knowledge of their success or otherwise), we then moved on to the highlight of the evening in the Long Room, plus coffee, and more drams for those who weren't driving.

One of the staff had prepared an excellent *This is Your Life* style book and presentation, followed at the end with the appearance of yours truly as the 'surprise' guest – dressed in the Hippo suit! This meant that I had to slip away and prepare for my arrival. Now ... I had spoken with the Busta House staff and they had suggested that I could change in the gents' toilet just opposite the Long Room and so be handy with the festivities.

Having been in the toilet before I thought things might be a trifle cramped but there being no other place that offered some degree of privacy this would have to be the choice. I nipped out to the car, got old Horace in his black bag and came back in and slipped quietly into the toilet. When inside, my worst fear was confirmed, there wasn't enough room to swing a cat, and a very small cat at that, never mind a 6ft+ Hippo. I made a mental note – *"Don't even think about inflating the suit until you get outside."*

Well, after having struggled to get the Sumo part of the suit out of the bag; left leg in, right leg in, take backside out of wash hand basin, crack head on light fitting, left arm in, right arm in, take foot out of toilet pan, connect up air compressor thing, find wires and battery pack, knock funny bone on door handle, jump (use the term loosely) up and down and rub fingers to get 'mirrly' feeling out of them, head-first into black bag again to locate furry part of suit, stand motionless while somebody tries door handle five, yes five, times (desperate for a pee I guess), same carry on, left leg, right leg, pick up cistern lid off floor, left arm, right arm, get blast of hot air in ear as accidentally set off electric hand drier, fasten full length Velcro strip on the belly, take foot out of waste paper basket ... then disaster ... I inadvertently knocked the 'ON' switch of the battery pack, and within seconds the suit was inflating – very quickly.

Possibly the confined space made things seem worse, but I was swelling so fast I began to become semi-wedged in the space between the toilet pan and the wash hand basin, and the ever encroaching walls.

Time to get out I concluded ... but easier said than done as the toilet door opened inwards. For the love o' God ... headlines on SIBC: 'Brae and Lerwick fire brigades called out to rescue a Hippo from the Busta House toilets'.

I was now fully wedged inside, couldn't get to the battery pack to switch the blasted thing off, and so had to open the door as far as I could and try and escape by squeezing through this narrow gap. Well, after a few desperate minutes I shot out of the toilet like a greyhound out of a trap and ricocheted off the opposite wall, slid slowly downwards and ended up in a heap at the foot. "Bloody Hell!" I muttered to myself, and looked around for the Hippo head. "Oh God," it was still in the toilet. Then I was aware of an elderly English couple, who I'd noticed previously sitting in the bar area having a light snack, standing open mouthed at the foot of the stairs.

"Good evening," says I. Well, what the hell can you say ... "Just having a wee spot of bother with this costume," ... "Nice place this, isn't it?"

"Oh, yes, very quiet and peaceful," she says! Poor souls. Imagine, they may have read the history of Busta House and the ghost story etc., but I don't think they were really ready for my explosive exit from the toilet.

Now I had to get up and this entailed rolling over onto my belly, drawing up the knees, backside high in the air and then standing upright ... not really the most elegant of manoeuvres! Anyway, we mastered that, and I managed to reach inside the toilet door, retrieve the head, then take up position just outside the Long Room, ready to sweep into the room at the given point.

If you know Busta House, then you'll know the Long Room is halfway between the bar area and the main outside door, and the timing of our little soiree meant that all the clientele who had been in the bar for supper now seemed to decide this was the time to go home. Marvellous ... here I am standing in the middle of the corridor, fully inflated in a Hippo suit, apparently on my own, not attached to anybody or any party, just nonchalantly leaning up against the wall, like I dress up in this way to go out for a meal every day!

"Oh, hello Magnie ... *What is du doing?*" the Aith High School lasses/teachers all out for a leaving party – one of their number was pregnant – we obviously bonded.

However ... all's well that ends well. I managed to get the timing right, remembered the step just inside the door, ducked to avoid losing the furry head as I came in, and danced around the room which, as the end of the *This is Your Life* piece had been quite emotional, seemed to lighten up the whole proceedings and rounded off the presentations. Got out of the suit, and bundled it all up again, and we all had an excellent night, plenty funs, and I drove home delivering my medics to their various houses and beds.

But, I resolved ... that is the last, Horace the Hippo is in the loft for good ... until the next time.

Tigger Two

I am drawn to the Disney Stores worldwide by some unknown magnetic force which propels me in through their open door and towards a sea of welcoming soft and squeezy toys. I have no control over this and have suffered the side effects for years now. None of these are too serious, but it has resulted in some awkward situations, not necessarily for me, but more for anybody in my close company or possibly mildly related to me.

In the heady days of summer I had purchased a small 'beanie' Tigger for my grandson, in the sure and certain knowledge he would appreciate the stripy, extroverted, bouncy, pouncy, flouncy character as much as his Granddad did. Over the ensuing weeks and months Tigger One took on a serious comforter role in his life, to the extent that he could not leave his side in moments of high drama, sad occasions and wildly excitable bath time events. This meant that Tigger One was washed numerous times, deliberately or otherwise, and so his stripes began to fade. Also, his mother spent many a fretful day constantly watching that Tigger One was not heaved out of the buggy, dropped on the Co-op floor, slipped out the car window and so maybe lost forever.

This resulted in Granddad being asked to look out for a 'back-up' for Tigger One – namely Tigger Two, the next time he was in Aberdeen. So began a normal Sunday morning, as normal as it can be for anybody suffering from Tigger Trauma. John Lewis was on the agenda for a search for some special lampshades and blinds etc., and I in turn was drawn by an insurmountable force ever nearer the lower floor of the Bon Accord Centre and towards the Costa Coffee stand at the foot of the escalators. However, on nearing the seating I felt myself being propelled across the floor and suddenly found myself inside the Disney Store.

After a few 'reccies' around the store, a fear began to grip me – there were no 'beanie' Tiggers to be found! Once more around the premises and more drastic action was called for, I resorted to getting down on all fours on the floor to check out the lower shelves thoroughly. As I crouched down on my hands and knees on the carpet I was aware of a small presence by my side and a little female voice said, *"What have you lost, Mister?"*

"Oh," says I, *"It's Tigger, he's gone missing, and I'm trying to find him,"* thinking that this small helper might have a better chance of glimpsing Mr T than me, as I bobbed my head up and down trying to see with the dreaded varifocals. After a couple of minutes I noticed there was another small person also bending down beside me, hands on knees, peering into the depths of the bottom shelves. *"What are we looking for?"* says he.

"Oh, this old man has lost his Tigger, and I'm helping him find it," says little Miss Information.

"Ok," replies small Mister Helper. *"What does he look like?"*

"It's TIGGER," says an indignant Miss Information. *"He looks like TIGGER,"* her voice rising possibly louder than I would have wanted.

This loud response brought some more little helpers to the scene and after a few minutes the situation was beginning to get a wee bit out of hand, as the 'old man' on all fours is crawling around the

Disney Store, head bobbing up and down as he tries to peer into the bottom shelves, followed closely by Miss Information loudly updating all around of our progress, while Mister Helper calls out the names of other animals and pulls them out onto the floor. Miss Information had by now recruited another lady friend who I took to be her younger sister, and so Miss Tidy was earmarked for clearing up duties, and she began to stack the heaps of soft toys Mister Helper had dragged out in a neat pile in the middle of the Disney Store. He in turn had enlisted the help of a close friend and ally, Mister Destroyer, who systematically wiped the floor with all the toys Miss Tidy had piled up in the aisles.

Further little people came and joined in the fun, followed at some point by bemused mothers and disapproving grandmothers who tut-tutted, as I tried to explain my mission. All this commotion brought out the ever-helpful Aberdonian assistants ... *"Fit are yee daein doon there, ye daft auld bugger? Kin yea nae see yer 'causin a hullabaloo in ma Store? Git up!"*

I had been so intent on seeking out Tigger that, although well aware there was a following of small people, I hadn't quite realised I had somewhere in the region of 10 to 12 bairns, squealing, giggling, shouting, crawling around, pulling out toys on the floor and causing general mayhem in a section of the shop. However ... among the many beanie toys that Mister Helper and Mister Destroyer had spread all around was ... Tigger Two. Woo Hoo!

At the same time as I spotted the little devil Miss Information did too, and she rushed across the floor, gathered him up in her arms and triumphantly presented me with him. So, there I was, now sitting among a sea of Eyeores, Piglets, Winnie-the-Poohs, Plutos, Mickey Mouses and a few more besides, clutching Tigger Two tightly to my chest. Success!

"Britney! ... Britney! Come here, dear." Miss Information's Mam had arrived to reclaim her daughter from the 'daft auld bugger' sitting on the floor. It may not have been 'Britney', but it was something of a similar vein. I thanked Miss Information profusely and, as I struggled to my feet, I explained my quest to the lead assistant – who I guessed,

judging by the make-up, was probably a former Miss Bon Accord 1982 – and helped return the beanies to the bottom shelf. Mister Helper and Mister Destroyer were nowhere to be seen, having made a speedy exit as soon as the fun had stopped.

I made my way to the checkout where assistant No. 2 smiled loudly at me and asked if there was anything else she could help me with. Well, thank you – I cannot say I saw much of this 'help' when I was on all fours previously madam!

Still, she threw in a free sheet of Disney Store wrapping paper, a small Disney Store gift bag, and a packet of red star confetti, as she tallied up my purchases. We exchanged pleasantries on the charms of Tigger Two, and parted friends, to the extent that she told me she hoped I'd come again. Her associate Miss Bon Accord, seemed less enthusiastic, but smiled the Disney Store smile at me, and wished me a 'Happy Day'!

I caught up with the rest of our party in the usual meeting place – outside the toilets next to Boots on the upper floor – and relayed my traumatic experience in securing Tigger Two.

They looked at me, shook their heads and said ... *"Do you like the colour of these lampshades?"*

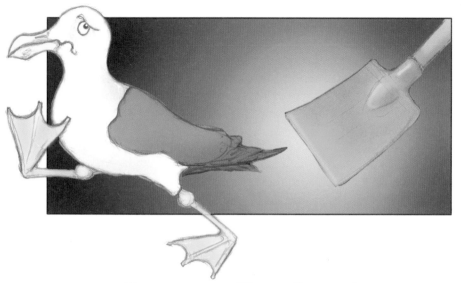

Sammy the Scorie

This little tale of a day in the life of Sammy the Scorie probably has more relevance to the town dwellers among you, as you will maybe see as the story unfolds.

Over the years the residents of Lerwick have enjoyed a harmonious if sometimes guarded relationship with the various feathered friends who co-habit the houses and gardens of this harbour town. Among them is the infamous seagull or 'scorie'. These seabirds have always been a permanent feature of the town and especially on the piers and quays along the waterfront.

However, over recent years they have taken to nesting in and around the rooftops of houses, mainly in the centre of the town, and as the young birds emerge their constant 'wheebing' begins to get on the residents' nerves until eventually they fly off into the wild blue yonder.

So it was that Sammy emerged into the delights of a Shetland summer and began his sojourn among the chimneys and rooftops of

Old Lerwick. It transpired one day that the weather took a bit of a turn for the worse and heavy deluges of rain fell upon the said rooftops, knocking young Sammy off his perch and down into the gardens below. At this stage in his development Sammy had not quite mastered the art of flying, or at least in any recognisable form, and so he wandered about the garden, head bobbing up and down, 'wheebing' loudly.

The residents of the house in question were enjoying a leisurely lie-in one morning when they were aware that the 'wheebing' seemed louder than usual. They both got up and checked the roof, but no sign of the offending birds could be seen and a further more intensive search was deemed necessary. After a while they discovered Sammy, performing his version of Riverdance in the back garden as he paddled his webbed feet up and down on the grass, bobbing about and 'wheebing' louder and louder. They tried chasing him away but he just paddled faster and came running back to them as soon as they turned their backs.

After a backyard consultation the decision was taken to phone the RSPB and seek their advice. *"Oh, he'll have fallen out of the nest, probably best to try and get him up off the ground, so the cats don't go for him,"* was the expert reply. Up off the ground? Hmmm ... No advice on how to achieve this was forthcoming, so various methods were considered and the man of the house cleverly devised a scheme whereby he would scoop Sammy up in a shovel and place him directly on the nearby shed roof, thus achieving the 'up off the ground' instruction.

So it transpired that Jim, as we'll call him, got out his trusty snow clearing shovel, coloured unobtrusively in a delicate shade of bright orange, and crept up on the unsuspecting Sammy. *"AH,"* a voice from the neighbouring garden called out. *"Great idea Jim, belt the little beggar over the head with a shovel, that'll maybe stop the bloody wheebing!"*

Possibly Sammy could understand a basic smattering of English or even just the tone was enough, but he got wind of the 'shovel-scheme' and paddled off at great speed around the garden as soon as Jim crept up behind him. Jim explained to his neighbour the intricacies of his 'shovel-scheme' and that in fact he was trying to help Sammy move to a higher place, not necessarily by belting him over the head but by moving him ever so gently up onto the shed roof. The neighbour was not entirely convinced of the success of this venture, in as much as he offered some salutary advice – *"Bigger fool de."*

So the afternoon wore on and Jim, now tiring of his efforts running around the garden chasing Sammy with a low level shovel and with the pain in his back beginning to wear him down a smidgen, decided that possibly this little rescue attempt was doomed to failure. He abandoned this scheme and again a team-talk was scheduled and further advice was sought from the so-called experts in the field. This time Mrs Jim phoned the RSPCA people at Gott and unfortunately they were not very helpful. In fact Mr RSPCA was on holiday so no information on the Sammy relocation front was available at all. Next on the list was the Hillswick Wildlife Sanctuary, who came good with some excellent advice. Sammy needed to get near a cliff, where he would instantly recognise the conditions and would launch himself off the cliff face and fly away as nature intended, free as a bird. Advice and instructions on how to capture Sammy, transport him to a nearby cliff, and launch him off into the exciting world of seabirds were all available from them too, and so a plan was hatched.

Late that afternoon, Jim and Mrs Jim had now gathered together the necessary equipment to capture and relocate Sammy, and they would then be able to spend a peaceful night without a wheeb or flechter in sight or sound.

The apparatus required for this operation consisted of a large bed sheet, a degree of physical dexterity and a sleight of hand equal to a member of the Magic Circle. So they both ventured outside again with the sheet spread out and slowly encircled Sammy, who had by now progressed to a boogie-woogie rhythm and was giving it his all in the far corner of the garden. This location was perfect for the capture routine of the master plan, and so Jim and Mrs Jim crawled nearer to Sammy. He slowed his fast paced dance routine to more of a sexy tango, and eyed the approaching antics of his landlords. At a critical moment Jim and Mrs Jim launched themselves on top of Sammy and rolled the bed sheet up quickly to secure him inside. A few hectic moments transpired as they grappled with the folds of the sheet and finally sat up exhausted by their efforts, but with a tight hold on the cloth.

Two beady eyes watched them, with its head cocked over to one side, and slowly launched into a new paddle routine, his little webbed feet just a blur – some 20 feet or so away on the other side of the garden! Sammy may be young, and maybe couldn't fly, but he could move with the speed of a bullet when sensing danger or some unknown aliens appearing to attack him.

After several attempts at this bed sheet plan, Sammy surely tired of the game and gave himself up, walking into the middle of the sheet, where he calmly stood while he was duly wrapped up tightly with just his head poking out through the cloth. Mrs Jim was detailed to hold him securely while they all climbed into the vehicle and headed off to the nearest cliffs – the Knab. Sammy appeared to enjoy the ride and sat looking out the window quite contentedly, drumming his feet happily on Mrs Jim's lap as they travelled through the town and up to the Knab.

On arriving at the Knab the next part of the plan was thoroughly rehearsed and discussed at length, while Sammy took in his new surroundings and uttered a few 'wheebs' at the many other seabirds flying in and around the cliffs. Mrs Jim carried Sammy to the wall and rather unceremoniously dumped him over the edge, onto the grassy ledge where he could contemplate flight and adventures anew among his many feathered friends who all lined up to watch the spectacle. Sammy ventured forth towards the cliff edge and had a good look up and down the cliff face, decided this was not something he was really ready for and wandered back to the dyke and looked up at Jim and Mrs Jim, gave a couple of long, loud wheebs and stood there. *"Dear God, what a bloody stupid bird,"* said Jim in exasperation, looking around for something to encourage

Sammy off the cliff. A few pebbles were found, and so it was that Jim and Mrs Jim stood leaning over the wall, throwing pebbles at Sammy the Scorie, who expertly dodged them all, set up a new dance formation and slowly but skilfully picked up the fallen pebbles in his beak, carried them to the rim of the cliff and dropped them over the edge, thus keeping his dancing area clear of any obstacles.

After half an hour or so of this, Jim and Mrs Jim decided they had done enough for Sammy and he was left to his own devices, and they set off home again, a whole day having been spent on Sammy's relocation process. However, they were happy in having achieved this and Sammy was now safe among his own kind, well out of the way of predatory cats, and he would soon learn to fly and seek out pastures new, far out to sea.

Sunday morning dawned bright and sunny, and having had a few beers the night before to celebrate their successful venture, Jim and Mrs Jim lay awake in bed and were planning a lazy day at home. Slowly Jim turned to Mrs Jim and said ... *"I don't ... believe it ... listen!"*

"Wheeb."

"Wheeb."

Sammy had indeed learned to fly ... ... straight back to their house!

Magnie's Wrastle
with the Flatpacks

Life was good. We'd managed to move in two days before Christmas, shifted a mountain of dust, a container load of personal belongings in numerous boxes, the cat had been released on parole from the Cattery for good behaviour and now, two months later, a semblance of order seemed to prevail.

True, our clothes were still strewn around various makeshift hangers and rails, in boxes, under beds and in Tupperware containers or suchlike. This was soon to be remedied however, as on a sunny Wednesday afternoon a large number of heavy, flat-shaped boxes had been delivered by two small grunting people.

These were the components of our new wardrobes and chest of drawers in an attractive shade of light maple, with two slim mirrored doors, a top shelf and two sets of hanging rails. The chest of drawers was a set of four, the top two being shallower than the larger and deeper lower two. They had looked so smart and fetching in the showroom, moved with the precision of a well engineered machine, and after a series of delicate measuring manoeuvres had been declared able to fit into the small but compact side room, part of our open-plan main bedroom. Just magic.

So it was on a Friday morning I set about opening the boxes in excited anticipation of at last finding a home for all our clothes etc. The small grunting people had been right, it would have been easier with a large crane and a forklift to move the boxes, rather than me and the cat alone. He helped by grabbing the ends of the cardboard and running backwards into the hallway. Eventually I managed to open and subsequently lay out all the laminated bits around the hall, the utility area, the kitchen, the bedroom, the dining room, the sitting room; and various small plastic bags containing hundreds of 'things' were positioned at strategic points around the house. Finally I found the instruction sheet. A wonder to behold. I always 'read' the instruction leaflets, as I have found to my cost over the years that no amount of DIY knowledge prepares you for the assembly of these objects.

Now I use the term 'read' loosely, as apparently this whole contraption was made in Germany and being a European nation they have conveniently written the instructions in Hindustani, Serbo-Croat, Afrikaans and a smattering of scribbles resembling ancient Egyptian, together with fourteen other nations none of whom apparently speak English. Exasperated already, I open the folded wonder once more and start again running my eye up and down, around and over the sections, looking for a happy familiar script.

Then, there it is ... all 66 lines of it, advising me that though they have made this thing to the very best of their ability, they take no responsibility for it being unable to fly, dive, paraglide, climb over unexplored terrain or ignite itself and destroy your home, your town, your city, your country etc. No mention of how to put together 114 pieces of MDF with 15 plastic packets containing modern day Lego bits and the off-cuts from an aircraft carrier. Ok, I did recognise a series of screws, but the rest was completely baffling.

I am not entirely new to this game, having re-constructed a kitchen from the infamous MFI units of the seventies, progressed through the decades to IKEA and so on, so I was not a total DIY Flat Pack Numpty, but the exploded innards of a wardrobe lying before me now seemed like something from the *Krypton Factor*.

More delving into the now discarded boxes – in which Elwood had decided to take up residence – revealed a further large sheet of paper with no writing on it all, just a series of pictures. Great stuff, instructions for plonkers. The very thing. Don't you just love the bit at the beginning where it shows you the finished article, a picture of two men or even, in this enlightened age, a man and a woman, one screwdriver and a large picture of a clock with the number '2' on it. This shows you that between you, you will be able to put the whole thing together with a screwdriver in two hours. Well, whoever drew that little diagram was a good few clowns short of a circus, that's for sure. Two hours! It's taken me the best part of an hour just to get inside the packaging, and I still don't know where we start. Ho Hum, time for a cuppa and a pleasant little browse through the pictures.

Right, we're off, renewed vigour and all that. Discovered the base and the top, the two sides and the centre section, together with the wiggly back panel. Where's Rolf Harris when you need him ... *"Tie me Kangaroo down sport, Tie me Kangaroo down ..."* – Whoop, Whoop.

This is number one, and the fun has just begun ... After half an hour of balancing on one leg while stretching to reach the top of the wardrobe panel, at the same time as screwing in the base section, we have a carcase. Woo Hoo! That wobble board of a back section was a challenge though. Just when you think you've got it slid into the narrow sections on the side channels, it pops out of the top or the bottom. You need to be an octopus with eight arms and legs to put this thing together. Never mind, we're there, and now having erected this in the bedroom area we have to shove it slowly backwards into position so that the front panels, doors, shelves, mirrors etc., etc can all be fitted.

So, here I am – picture this – down on all fours, pushing slowly the whole heavy unit back in towards the wall, where there is about a couple of inches clearance at each side. I resemble a sort of desert marsupial with my nose to the floor, and my backside high in the air.

My helper, meanwhile, is steadying the whole contraption so that it doesn't tilt forwards and flatten me into the new off-white carpet. The bloodstains are hellish to remove. *"Heh ... Wait a minute, I have to get out of here!"* a muffled cry emerges from behind the unit.

Uh Huh ... In my supreme efforts to position the wardrobe I had been edging it up towards the back wall with great gusto, forgetting she was slowly being crushed between the unit and the wall. *"Come out of there."*

"I'm trying!" Now she's a neat person and slim of build, but try as she might she wasn't going to squeeze through the 4" gap between the unit and the side wall. Ok, the desert marsupial now goes in reverse, hauling said unit behind it. Eventually she emerges from behind the thing, slightly distressed as the realisation dawns that she might have been trapped in there for days, with only a cream cracker and a Kraft cheese slice being able to be passed through the narrow gap.

Ok, we're away again. Nose down, push, push, Wha-Hey it's there. Great. Time for another cuppa as we size up the door panels, the aircraft bits and the assorted 57 varieties of screw needed to locate these items to the carcase.

Find the correct doors, get them on the floor, attach the necessary bits which make up the hinges and the sliding door thing, the adjustment screws and the door handles etc. Slowly lift the heavy frigging door into position and slide it onto the carcase hinge section. Stand back and admire. Door slips forward a fraction then shoots out of the hinges, cracks me on the head and lands on my right foot. *"Oh you naughty, naughty door,"* I remark while jumping around the room, rubbing my head and foot at the same time. This is not entirely a good idea, as my balance is momentarily out of synch with the earth's gravitational movement. The resulting mess of legs and arms rolling about the floor closely resembles a camel on crack, and is not a pretty sight.

After extricating myself from this surreal situation, I decide a further investigation of the offending door and frames are needed. Study the pictograms and count the number of little holes on each side. Ah Hah … there's something not quite right here. Some little holes are at the bottom when they should be at the top, and some little holes are also at the back when they should be at the front. The stupid German tossers have drilled the holes in the wrong places! Uh Uh … wait a minute, if I take this centre section and … turn it … Oh no, surely not. Yes, you big Wally, the centre section of the carcase is in the wrong way round, upside down in fact!

Marvellous. How in the name of the Father do we sort that without taking the whole blessed thing to bits again? This is a low point in the proceedings, a very low point. Wardrobes? Who wants wardrobes anyway? What was wrong with the plastic rails from Argos, the Tupperware boxes, the … yea, yea, ok. Bit of head scratching and maybe, just maybe, if I undo the screws at the top and bottom, do a bit of shoogling here and there, maybe even a bit of shoving there, followed by a certain restrained but calculated thumping here, it might, just might, all go back in again?

A half hour passes, Elwood's sitting with his ears pinned back, his eyes resembling a Japanese Kamikaze pilot, flattened to the floor in eager anticipation of the whole thing exploding in a myriad of pieces – but no – clunk, click it all goes together again. That's a fluke, but thank God for that. This is a high point in the proceedings, a very high point.

Now the doors are offered up again. Into the hingey bits, screwed tight, the sliding/folding door sections are coupled up and a thing that looks like it could be the main piece from a nuclear reactor is connected to the door via an aluminium rail bit, which is similarly connected to the shelf via the side panel and the plastic guide wheel is snapped into position while the side adjustment screw is millimetre by millimetre eased out to compensate for the tidal movement in the North Sea. Closer inspection reveals that the apparent tilt is due to my left slipper, which has somehow got trapped underneath the frame. How the hell did that get there?

Possibly during the dromedary break-dancing session on the floor earlier on, I guess, it must have been thrown outwards by the centrifugal force of my legs and wedged itself underneath.

"*Can you come and help me, please?*" As I push on the top she cleverly whips out the offending slipper and balance is restored again. Ok, just another three doors to go. It's a doddle really. Two hours later we have the second door in place. Getting these two sets of doors lined up, and able to open without catching in the floor, the walls, the side panels themselves, is an art form in itself. No small pictograms for this operation – you're on your own buddy!

Darkness descends, as the intrepid flat packer carries on determined to succeed. At this rate we could be finished by Tuesday. Another couple of hours later, we have the second two sets of doors in place – that's 100 per cent faster than previously. The guy's a genius. We've also managed to take in food and liquids in this period, watch *Tigger and the Amazing Honey Pot* on the 'Play Disney' channel (a new and exciting discovery) and engage Elwood in a bout of martial arts. He wins as usual, springing off the top of the sideboard catching me unawares and unprepared for this rearguard assault. Cheat.

Four small pins slotted into holes and the shelves are in place. Getting the hang of this now. The clothes rails are carefully positioned to allow for shirts and trousers that look as if designed for a gorilla and a giraffe respectively. The other side is filled with clothes that seem more normal and proportioned. We close the doors and admire the effect. It seems to fit, it doesn't fall over, the doors operate, the hangers slide effortlessly. All's well. An hour passes and we are aware of a faint cry for help, a sort of muffled *miaooowww*. Tracked through the house to the wardrobes, a door is opened and a disgruntled, annoyed cat emerges from the gloom. He haughtily strides out through the bedroom door, tail high in the air, and demands to be let outside.

Tomorrow it's the turn of the chest of drawers, but that holds no fear after today. A small picture of two men and a clock with a '1' on it. Yeah ... right!

Aeroplane Ablutions

As I see it. this world is made up of people who fit into aeroplane toilets and those like me who don't. Now it's not for want of trying, believe you me, I have squeezed myself into a variety of cubicles designed to house small furry animals rather than humans, with the avowed intention of relieving myself of surplus fluids etc., and suffered badly for it.

What character drew up a plan for a room that has no window, a curved sloping ceiling, a door the size of a small coffee table, has various sharp pointy things sticking out of the walls, and a geyser of boiling hot water all crammed into a space resembling a corn flakes packet?

No doubt Mr Boeing, or whoever, thought it a jolly little wheeze to put a toilet in the front and rear compartments of a cigar tube, as there was obviously more money to be had in shoving a series of seats designed for legless dwarves into the main section of the fuselage than allowing any room for human ablutions.

The whole process of actually going to the toilet on a plane opens up a huge range of emotions not naturally experienced in everyday life. Often you are the person sitting in the window seat, and so, after having been mildly frightened by the emergency lecture, lifejacket demonstration, take off procedure – in which, in your informed opinion, the pilot left it far too late to actually pull the handles up – you swallowed a vodka and coke way too fast. The outcome of this and previous numerous coffees is the accumulation of fluid in your body which is now being forced downwards and you need to visit the toilet compartment. Excellent.

You have a peek over the top of the seat in front to locate the nearest watering hole and see it way down the aisle near the pilot's playroom, and so a strategy is considered on the best way to approach this area. The woman sitting next to you has fallen asleep with her magazine, cardigan, pen and empty crisp packets on her lap, with the table pulled down in front of her. The guy in the outer or aisle seat appears to be having a small seizure and is twitching quite violently at times, and you have to negotiate a passage over the top of them both.

After a couple of prods the woman stirs, looks at you in fear and alarm as you point to the aisle, gesticulating wildly, and eventually gets the message and gathers all her belongings together and stands half up in the seat. You claw your way along the top of the seats in front as you edge past, slapping the people in front around the forehead as you grab hold of anything to steady your balance. The guy at the end is still in convulsions and no amount of poking is having any effect. Just then you notice a white lead running down from his head and you realise this comedian is keeping time to the music on his iPod. With a quick flick you pull the cord from his ears, this enacts an instant response, the convulsions stop, the eyes open and he mouths some obscenity at you as again you point frantically at the aisle. Once more the meaning of the signals bears fruit and he grabs his iPod and clambers out of his seat letting you step into the aisle bent over like a half shut knife.

You edge your way forwards, avoiding stray legs, games and brown furry animals belonging to assorted bairns, and head down towards the front of the plane and the toilet, concentrating on holding in as best you can. A couple of seconds later you bring up in the front of a metal trolley being propelled up the aisle by Nigel and his partner Rodney ... *"Coffee, Tea or Milk."* Oh, for goodness sake, we don't have time for this. A spot of navigation is required here as they stand their ground, unreceptive to your pleading for a way through. Oh well, that's it then, you squeeze into the space occupied by a small child in the aisle seat to let Nigel and Rodney past, as the little treasure spears you in the leg with his latest Lego Duplo skyrocket. Eventually you get back out into the aisle and proceed to the toilet where on arrival there is a queue of assorted people all waiting to get into the cupboard.

The light panel with the red cross on it is on, proclaiming to all and sundry that somebody is in there, so you join the queue and wait as patiently as you can. Eventually a large woman and two, yes two, small children emerge looking a tad flustered to say the least. How in the name of the Father did they all get in there, and best of all manage to do what they had to do and make it back still in one piece? Beats me. No wonder she's looking like she's just gone ten rounds with Mike Tyson.

Next in line is a quiet looking fellow who I'm guessing has never flown before, let alone been inside a plane's toilet compartment – boy is he in for a surprise! After a short spell where he attempted to push the door inwards he finally pulls it open and disappears inside – a couple of seconds later suddenly the door shoots open and he sticks his head out and looks around. Seems quite amazed to see us all standing there looking at him, he nods at no one in particular and disappears inside once more. This happens a further three times and I'm guessing he's looking for the light switch – which of course doesn't exist – and finally he must have decided to try and do the business in the dark. Eventually the red 'occupied' light comes on, so he's finally managed to lock the door and, all going well, all will be illuminated for him now.

An eternity seems to pass while you shuffle on and off a leg waiting desperately and just then you hear a muffled cry from within – ah, yes, he's discovered the hot water taps. Another while passes then out he comes, after shaking the door violently from within for a good two to three minutes before he obviously remembered he'd locked it. What appears bears no resemblance to what went in and I struggle to recognise the apparition that materialises. The glasses are all askew, the hair is standing completely on end, he is minus one shoe which he is carrying in his left hand and, best of all, his jumper is now on back to front. What on earth has he been doing? Maybe Mike Tyson or another small gorilla *is* in there.

Finally it's my turn and in we go ... Crack, that's the first, as my head bounces off the opposite wall. I'm heading in facing the offending wall and now have to turn round and lock the door in the dark. At 6ft 3" I'm not excessively tall – statistically average European males are slowly catching up with me at between 5ft 11" and 6ft 1" – so you wouldn't have thought a couple of inches or so would have made that much difference. The designers have obviously planned the compartments around the African pygmy who leap in at around 4ft nothing, or possibly a rather tall meerkat. Whatever, the next five minutes or so would have given Harry Houdini a run for his money.

Dear God, what a performance. After struggling to stay upright while bent over holding on to the wall, the sink, the door, and various pieces of my anatomy, I manage to relieve myself in the proper receptacle and then I push the 'flush' button. Well ... just let me warn you, make sure you're holding onto some substantial piece of the aircraft, like the wing or the tail-plane, before you push that vacuum button. This machine can suck the fillings out of your teeth as well as empty the pan in three seconds flat. Never ever stand with your back to it unless you have a desire to walk like a penguin for the rest of your life. They're weird those things. Having survived the vacuum attack I then attempt to wash my hands in the yoghurt tub they call a basin. The first challenge is to turn on the taps, and as they are similar to those automatic ones you find in public toilets worldwide you wouldn't think it was too much of an ordeal. Wrong!

These ones are designed to put out fires like Red Adair does on oil platforms, and have the force of ten water cannons linked together in unison. I tentatively push down on them for nothing to happen, and then try a bit harder while standing as far back as I can from the basin in case of the dreaded splashback, but still no luck. Eventually I push down that little bit harder again and ... For the love of God, what a mess! It's all over the walls, the floor, the door, and, of course, the front of my newly purchased chinos, not to mention my glasses as well. I frantically wipe my trousers down with what's left of the toilet/tissue paper that's not a soggy mess, and crack my head once again on the coom ceiling.

Trying to straighten myself up and dry my hands on my shirt I finally compose myself as best I can, turn the lock back and emerge into the main compartment with a jaunty smile, and swan off down the aisle as nonchalantly as I can while exposing my soaked chinos to everybody sitting at waist level. The eyes of all 280 passengers on this 757 are glued to me as I wander about looking for my seat, and finally I see the 'Twitcher' and his partner 'Nora Batty' eyeing me up from afar and they graciously half stand to let me in past them. Once again I use an elderly gentleman's ears in the seat in front as grab handles and safely make it to the window seat.

Exhausting and mentally draining, there can be fewer more traumatic events than a visit to an aeroplane toilet ... unless, of course, you've showered in a NorthLink cabin ...

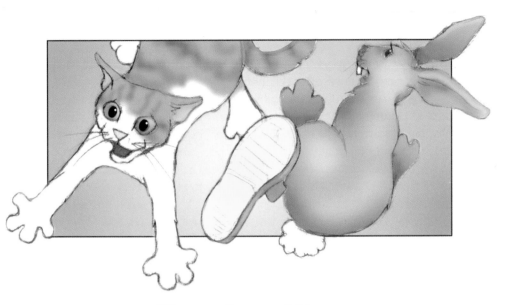

Cloudspotting

I recall it was a Tuesday morning, and it dawned a fine bright day with numerous cloud formations rising slowly above the horizon. As I sat and munched my way through my cereal, truttled at the radio, discussed the current financial crisis at some length with Elwood the cat – who I have to say has some pretty innovative ideas to solve the situation, but I just know nobody will take him seriously – I chanced upon a cloud shape which resembled a famous mouse and I thought it needed capturing on film.

As we have a Rayburn in our kitchen which means we are cosy-cosy most of the time, and being the ageing hippie that I am, during the summer I generally pad around the house barefoot or in flip-flops, so I spanged off the kitchen stool to grab the camera and head off outside to capture the moment for posterity. Flip-flops and speed are not very compatible items, and as I skittered on the wooden floor, Elwood, who was in his *'I am not to be disturbed position'* clapped up alongside the Rayburn door, became aware of a large out of control presence bearing down on him. He awoke, wide eyed, and with the speed of a bullet shot right across the front of me as I made my way to the opening between the kitchen and the sitting room.

This resulted in him being clipped around the back legs, which altered his flight path considerably and he ricocheted off the waste bin into the kitchen wall and cannoned back into the Rayburn. A loud wail emitted from him as he bounced around the room, spitting at the bin, the Rayburn and me all at the same time. Stupid cat – he should have known I was nowhere near him. I in turn burst through the opening like some crazed terrorist, equally wide eyed and single flip-flopped as the errant left one shot past me while my arms wind-milled in an attempt to stay upright.

I was minutes away from certain death, or at least serious injury, when I managed to catch hold of the dining table chair and though it certainly helped to slow my downward spiral I managed to pull it over on top of me and together we gracefully landed on the floor amid a mess of chairs, cats, cushions, and curses. I am now lying on the floor seeing the beautiful clouds through the window and remarkably it's still there ... Mickey – or maybe Minnie – Mouse. Two ears, a round head and an upturned nose – just magic!

Now just briefly imagine the scene here ... a long lanky buffoon of the highest calibre is spread-eagled on the floor, a half set of flip flops dangling from one foot, a loose cushion still attached to a dining room chair which is upturned on top of him and a bemused Elwood, who is now flat on the floor in 'poised to strike' mode, and we look at each other eye to eye.

Hmmmm ...

Remarkably, I suffer no injuries and as I extricate myself from this position I start to giggle, and this in turn defuses the cat attack and he slopes off back to the Rayburn to adopt his 'just cooking' position. I clamber up and get the camera out of the drawer, slip on the left flip flop and head off out the patio door to capture this exciting cloud formation.

Now time is of the essence here as clouds, as you will know, do not last, and a few minutes can alter a shape considerably, so I am concentrating on getting the camera switched on, the lens open etc., and I just don't see the rabbit!

Rabbits are funny animals – like funny peculiar – they freeze when startled or in any danger, in the daft idea that whatever is approaching/attacking them cannot see them. Well, they were right on that point – no question about that! I am now fast approaching Tufty the Rabbit at speed, my radar is not switched on, I am in head down, do not stop, do not pass go, mode ... and subsequently clatter into the bloody thing.

I never saw Tufty till he sort of drop kicked past me. I, meantime, carried on, as momentum does to you, and overtook him in a dive Michael Phelps would have been proud of. Preservation of life and soul took priority but I held on to the camera and kind of ploughed into the grass, swept past Tufty who had a dazed quizzical look on his face, and at this point, if you can imagine, the rabbit's brain clicked in and in a flash this thought was going through it ... *"What the hell was that? Here I was just sitting with my back to the house – safe in the knowledge The Cat was inside – nibbling away at the chickweed, when WAAOOMPH, a tornado came out of nowhere, catapulted me six feet in the air, a flip flop wrapped itself around my ears and this idiot cartwheeled past!"*

The two of us sat there on the grass, not three feet apart, eyeing one another up, and both thinking – *Dear God, what a plonker ...!* You only realise that rabbits can giggle when you're up close like that.

Now I surely have the inherent survival instincts of the wooga-wooga bird or some such endangered species, and survive I did, but now Mickey was beginning to float away but I finally got the snap of the cloud formation I had been looking for. You have to use your imagination to spot these shapes in the sky, and a certain degree of dexterity not to mention physical flexibility.

Cloudspotting – it's not always as dangerous as this, so the next sunny day when the sky is full of candy floss clouds, lie down on your back, empty your mind and see what you see. Cartoon characters, hippos on skateboards, flying saucers, the list is endless. Just remember, don't do it while you're driving. Not a good idea.

Mamoosa & Me

Glasses, or spectacles, and I have had a tempestuous relationship over the years. We first met way back in the early sixties when, having managed to fall over the cliffs at the Waari Geo, I damaged the nerve in one eye, resulting in a fairly serious loss of vision. Nowadays with all the clever laser treatments available no doubt it could have been repaired, but back then you just got on with it.

After a period of walking round in circles as I adjusted to the lack of peripheral vision, I was duly introduced to spectacles. These were, if you can recall the heady fashion of those days, round, brown framed lenses with sort of semi-circular pink legs which wrapped themselves around your ears, ensuring they stayed on during football, hand stands, tornados and such like. No designer FCUK or Police styles then-a-days, just the basics. However well attached they were, somehow or other they would break or a lens would fall out and temporary repairs with Elastoplast or similar was called for.

So, as the years progressed I must have worked my way through loads of pairs of glasses and, of course, fashion now plays a part whereby you change them as the styles change if you are so inclined. Contact lenses, or lens in my case, would possibly solve this entire problem but somehow I've never got into them, partly because the idea of poking your finger in your eye every day didn't appeal much and also, in the early days all that cleaning etc., seemed a tad unnecessary. A quick breath and wipe with your shirt tail solved the seeing glitch in a moment with glasses.

One of the hazards of wearing glasses is painting; painting walls and ceilings with a roller, especially. This can manifest itself into major crises at times. I have a habit of being quite a vigorous painter of walls and ceilings, in the thought that the more paint I can load onto the roller the more I will cover, and therefore the faster I will finish the blessed job. This works admirably and in no time I can step back and admire all the holidays in the sections I've missed. More vigorous painting and this is soon covered up and we're finished. The boiler suit is spattered from top to bottom, the old shoes are liberally coated with a myriad of colours from previous DIY sessions, and of course the glasses and what little hair is left on the head have taken their share of this coating too. This results in vivid hallucinations when viewed in the bathroom mirror, depending on the colour scheme.

This was the scenario a few weeks ago. When helping to paint out shop premises I had been overly enthusiastic in my attempts to finish the job on time and the resulting white paint covering the walls, ceilings and me had left the glasses badly spattered. The following morning in a rush to get out I had popped the glasses on and realised then that they were very heavily coated, so I nipped through to the kitchen where the green sponge lay next to the sink and, rinsing the spectacles under the hot water, proceeded to give them a quick scrub. Now, as you will understand I obviously didn't have my glasses on and so my sight was somewhat impaired. Just to make sure I had cleaned them thoroughly I gave them an extra good rub, wiped them dry in the paper towel and popped them on. I couldn't see. Not a thing. Nothing but grey mist everywhere. What the hell? Oh, for the love of God ... I'd rubbed them with the back of the green sponge, the bit with the coarse covering designed to remove fired-on grease, diesel, nuclear waste etc. from frying pans ... not for use on thin plastic lenses. Not ever. Uh-Huh.

This is when you are always glad you kept your last pair of prescription glasses, even if they are two or more years out of date, as having learned over the years that the occasional break or damage happens, you still need to see. But the question now is ... where in heavens name did you put them away 'safely'? A lot of *"Can you mind where I said I was going to put my old glasses?"* questions get asked, and a lot of rummaging around in the most unlikely spots takes place, and after an hour or so of frantic searching you find the pair from three eye tests ago. There is no sign of the pair from the last time whatsoever. Oh so, they'll do.

You pop them on ... Dear God, did you really wear these? They seem like they are the size of small dustbin lids and while not entirely focussed your eyes, or eye in my case, will adjust in time. Time to visit the optician again. After a fortnight, the new pair arrives and once again your eyes take a day or so to adjust to the varifocals, and the bridge of your nose and your ears take a pounding, but eventually all is well and full vision is restored to normal.

For the first time in weeks I was home at night and on this occasion home alone. No painting, varnishing, woodchip removal, flat-packing etc., so I thought I would cook myself something different, pour a glass of vino, watch Liverpool destroy Arsenal, enjoy a DVD and just have a night off completely. Sometimes 'home alone' is actually very good, I'm a people person (in case you didn't know this) and I need and love one-to-one company or just to be in a crowd some of the time, but occasionally just by yourself is really pretty good too. No distractions, no hassle, just do your own thing.

I decided the menu would be something I'd never cooked before, but it had to be simple and quick, so scoured the *Good Food* mags and found an Indo-Iraqi-Jewish veggie snack called Potato Mamoosa (I think that's the spelling). Now you may know exactly what that is but in case not it's a chilli, diced potato, turmeric, coriander & paprika spiced, red onion and tomato mix with beaten eggs scrambled in it at the end. All very good but I thought it could do with some extra meatiness, so I tossed in some chorizo sausage slices for a bit more flavour and that seemed to do the trick. Maybe not quite the essence of the vegetable snack it was meant to be but something different, that's for sure.

So, plate in hand, glass o' vino and DVD remote in the other I sat down to watch *Madagascar – Escape 2 Africa*. Good, but not as good as the original we thought. That's we, as in Elwood and me. This is the point when he discovered I had got my new glasses. Do you ever notice that cats are actually hugely observant, as against dogs that sniff at everything but take nothing in? Elwood had been lying in his usual upside-down-reveal-all position on the mat and on the arrival of the said food etc. into the room, rolled over and ambled across to sniff the air and discuss the merits of the aforementioned menu.

At this point he sat down on the floor and eyed me face to face ... I was acutely aware then of a large wide-eyed steady stare as he took in my new glasses. This stare lasted a long while and then he slowly stretched, clambered up onto the settee and poked his face right up to mine and we were now inches apart as he surveyed the new glasses intimately. Then I saw the eyes slanting, the ears going back, but too late, he was too fast for me and in a flick he had pawed them clean off my face and into the Potato Mamoosa. He never moved an inch, just stood there and stared at my glassless face and then, satisfied that he had got rid of the offending articles and life had been restored to normal, he sauntered off the settee and back down onto the mat. I meanwhile had to rescue my chillies, egg, tomato, and onion-encrusted glasses and head for the sink to wash off the food. No scrubbing of the lenses this time thankfully but just a quick hose down.

I returned to the scene of the attack and again settled down to eat my dinner, he in turn rolled over, saw the glasses were back on and once again swiftly climbed the settee and took up the eyeball to eyeball position. This is quite disconcerting when you're trying to relax and eat a culinary delight of your own making. Having a large cat staring directly at you with that wide-eyed gaze, just inches from your face, knowing full well that he may easily pounce in seconds, tends to make you a trifle uneasy. I edged further away across the settee, but the trooker followed me step by step across the sofa.

Finally I had reached the edge and could go no further. He growled at this stage. Think I have possibly mentioned this phenomenon before, whereby he imitates a full grown American Grizzly to great effect. I whipped off the glasses just before he pawed them off a second time, and satisfied he had achieved a result he once again turned round and shoved his butt in my face ... why do cats always do that? Finally he ambled off the sofa and back to the mat, giving me a full stare just to check I hadn't slipped them back on again.

Possibly this is why I thought *Madagascar 2* was not quite as good as the original. Seeing it through a blurred haze is not always the best viewing option. The rest of the night was a battle of wits between us as I attempted to put the glasses on and off, while he checked periodically and growled to show his disapproval.

The 4-4 game at Anfield was good, what I saw of it, but had to re-watch on Sky Sports to see Arshavin score four and Torres & Co's beauts. The highs and lows of that game had me squirming and elated in equal measures. Emotionally drained and needing company to share those moments, Elwood was no substitute for a best friend and his displeasure at my latest purchase didn't help matters one iota. Finally he condescended to accept the new apparition before him as he made one last close-up inspection, sniff and gentle pawing to test the quality of the product. Presumably chillies, tomato and onion flavoured glasses are ok, as they ultimately got his seal of approval and a gentle purring as he lay beside me confirmed his acceptance.

The conclusion I've reached is that while 'home alone' may well seem a great idea in principle the actual reality sometimes never quite matches up to the dream, and never, ever, share it with a 'picky' cat.

Quasimodo Meets the Japanese

Sometimes folk say, *"We never have eventful holidays like you"*, but the truth is we don't actually plan these little events, they just seem to happen and while I'm not one who gets fazed by much, possibly this helps to make me see the funny side of it all.

What started out as a short break to visit relations in Holland, and then onto Barcelona for five nights, proved to be a little adventure in a way, though it was all hugely enjoyable and did in no way mar the occasion.

We had a glorious run down on the NorthLink ferry to Aberdeen and after the usual battle with the wet shower curtain and the soap container in the pint sized cabin toilet, I shot out of there washed, shaved and clean, if a little traumatised by the whole experience. Off to catch the train to Edinburgh and an overnight stay there and a chance to visit our nephew and his family before catching the Easyjet flight to Amsterdam.

By opting for the *'Speedy Boarding'* service on this flight, I managed to secure the emergency seats for us and so languished in the delights of extra legroom and was able to spread out my 6ft 3" frame relatively easily. Again we had an excellent flight and munched away on a hot panini and drank a bottle of red wine during the journey and landed at Schiphol about 10 minutes ahead of schedule.

So far so good, and as Schiphol is a massive airport it was a long walk to the baggage carousel after clearing passport control. We duly arrived there to find our cases merrily spinning around awaiting us and this was the moment when things went a little bit pear shaped. Being tall of stature my back has always been a source of annoyance ever since an accident climbing the 'banks'. So much so, that it occasionally 'clicks' out at the slightest thing and with no warning, and as I leaned over to pluck our cases from the carousel I felt it 'click' and there I was, like a half shut knife again. Superb. Here we were at the start of the holiday with our cases rolling round and round the Schiphol baggage area and no visible means of retrieving them. Eventually between us we got them off and onto the floor and, thankfully, as they are the type with wheels at the rear we could trundle them until we found an airport trolley to take them out to the car park.

We were met by our relations and we headed off to their house and a much needed rest and a meal, as well as the usual catch up on all things newsy or pertaining to family and Shetland.

Next morning we planned a visit to the world famous Keukenhof Gardens just outside Amsterdam, and with a fine day in prospect I stocked up on painkillers and we set off. The gardens are truly remarkable with an amazing range of flowers, trees and bushes, plus a beautiful walking area all around the park with lakes and birds etc.

We had gone a piece and though sore, my back was not too bad and I ambled, shuffled, wobbled along in the rear. They all commented on my unusual gait, and so, as you do, I started imitating the Hunchback of Notre Dame, Quasimodo. I swayed violently behind them with my left arm trailing on the ground, loudly wailing, *"The Bells, The Bells"*. Within a few minutes the hundreds of folks that appeared to be following us suddenly vanished and the ladies, having taken a digital photo of the wild eyed 'stalker' following them, revealed the extent of the mass exodus as on viewing the picture there was a huge dearth of visitors. Hmmm ...

The next day we headed for the Kroller-Muller Park in south-east Netherlands, near Arnhem, where among other things there is a world famous art museum with a large collection of Vincent van Gogh paintings. After having cycled around the park and enjoyed a small snack we then cycled off to the museum and had a look around the famous galleries. By this time my back was beginning to complain and as we came into a quiet section of the gallery I espied a large, low bench set directly in the middle of the viewing area. Magic. The very thing for sore backs. I shuffled up to it and lay very gingerly down on top, with my legs dangling over the edge. Slowly I leaned back and closed my eyes and as I lay there breathing shallowly but steadily, the pain began to subside and I was in peace.

After a short while I was aware of movement around me and a loud voice suddenly starting shouting, *"Ahh ha, yo soom tung Van Gogh ... lee ming ho tao ..."* or some such thing. I lay perfectly still and slowly opened my eyes. I was surrounded by around 20 elderly Japanese who were being led by a large Sumo type lady waving a long stick with a red ribbon on it. She was the source of the noise. They were obviously being shown round the sacred hall of Van Gogh and seemed ill-prepared for the 6ft European mammal resting in the middle of the famous artworks. I struggled to get up and that was possibly my first mistake, as I very nearly cleaned three of them off their feet as I swung around on the bench, my legs flaying away through the air as I tried to pull myself up to a sitting position. Eventually I abandoned this idea and just slumped over onto the floor, onto my knees, and hauled myself up to what is laughingly called an upright stance. This seemed to scare them even more and

Ms Sumo and party shot off round the corner, and they never did seem to appreciate the full value of Vincent's *'Old Man in Sorrow'* hanging on the wall above me.

The rest of the Dutch experience was great. We had a canal tour on a large boat which was rammed by another canal barge as she sped through under a bridge, and that fairly livened up the whole experience, especially for the skipper's dog who was lying sleeping on the gunwale at the time, and very nearly ended up in the canal. Two pickpockets sitting alongside us were arrested by four plain clothes police-people who jumped them. Obviously they had been stalking the two culprits for a considerable while, and I had noticed this guy acting strangely for a time, talking into his shirt and glancing furtively all around him, standing up and down etc., and had made a mental note to avoid sitting next to him on the canal tour. Little did I realise he was the policeman! The spaced out kid was sitting quite quietly right next to me!

We appeared to be doing Europe alphabetically, as having managed to get out of Amsterdam without further incident we headed for Barcelona, via the Spanish budget subsidiary of Iberia, Clickair. No, I have no idea either, unless it was some marketing guy's idea of a good name for an online airline? Once again we had an excellent flight, with nice food, good wine and no episodes with small milk containers or the latest in-catering facilities brainchild 'Dairy Stix'. Have you seen these, little tubes of milk where you tear off the end and pour the contents into your tea or coffee? Clever! We arrived on time at the very large but pleasant Barcelona airport and having secured a taxi sped off into the city and our hotel, accompanied by a running commentary on all things Spanish, good and Barcelona wise, by our excellent driver.

This visit was, thankfully, largely uneventful and my back had by now become quite supple again as the lower muscles and ligaments finally relaxed and took in the scenery etc., like the rest of me. We had an excellent five nights in this exciting city, which caters for all tastes. There are marvellous art and architecture sights, great food, wine and tapas bars, street entertainers, classy Spanish senoritas, a smattering of fruitcakes and a few out and out nutters all thrown in for good measure. On top of this there is Las Ramblas to explore, the old city haunts, the promenade and harbour, plus a very attractive beach. It can be as pricey or as cheap as you want it to be and thankfully there are very few Roast Beef, Full English Breakfast and *Daily Star* Cafes, if any, to be found anywhere within the city.

One of the highlights was the discovery that our room in the hotel contained a Jacuzzi. Now, in all the exciting adverts for one of these machines you see a happy, starry-eyed couple sitting together in their Jacuzzi, softly flickering candles arrayed around them, silky bubbles slowly rising and falling as they sip romantically on silver flutes of champagne. However, Mrs S declared she was not intending to partake of this device either alone or together, as on our early inspection of the room, prior to reading any of the information booklets, I had pushed the buttons on the bath panels (as you do) and caused what seemed like a small earthquake to shake the room, the hotel and possibly a sizeable area of Barcelona. On closer inspection of the instructions on the wall, they conveyed the warning: *"You are kindly requested not to switch on the engine until the water covers your six holes, in order to avoid the entrance of wind."*

I have never had occasion to ride in one of these contraptions before and so, always up for a challenge, I decided on our last night at the hotel that I would venture into the bathroom intent on a relaxing wallow with the gentle vibrations soothing my old back in readiness for the journey home the next day. I strictly adhered to the instructions on the holes and nearly drowned in the process, lying down as the water slowly covered all my orifices, though on reflection I think they meant the six holes in the sides of the bath. They also kindly supplied an assortment of liquid soaps, bubble bath, and fragrant flower water, with all labels written in Spanish. I unscrewed the caps and sniffed, but as I didn't understand what the contents were and was largely undecided on which were the soaps and which the essence of rose petals etc., I just heaved the lot in as they were really quite small containers. Not one of my better ideas. On switching on the creature, within seconds the bath was a mass of pink foamy bubbles rising like some huge marshmallow, accompanied by a tsunami of equally large proportions, with the water ranging from side to side of the tub in an enormous tidal wave. There is some power in the engines I must say! Suddenly I could see a problem looming as this foamy animal began to take over the whole bathroom, escaping from the tub and beginning to envelop everything inside. Could I find the stop button? No way. It was located as far back behind me as was humanly possible, probably in a handy spot for the person seated in the bath surrounded by low level waist high foamy water. At this point the foam was now well above my head and I was fighting for air. There was only one thing for it. I took a large breath and dived into the soapy mass ploughing my way through the solid wall of bubbles and, after what seemed like an eternity as I slid and slipped, I finally managed to smack the button hard and stop the beast. Well ... it took me most of an hour to wipe down the walls and the ceiling, and when I at last found the mirror and saw myself I figured I closely resembled Mr Blobby, covered as I was in pink foam from head to foot. Dear o' dear, for such a carry on. I had to lie down for a while after all that, though in hindsight the whole experience was quite exciting, if a trifle dangerous. I think in future I may test the soaps etc. in the hand washbasin first by giving them a fast 'swittle', just to determine how ferocious they can become, or possibly I'll just stick to the shower.

Kittimas Decorations

Now, I love Christmas. I don't know if this is a normal male thing or just a passing phase, but for nigh on sixty years I have always enjoyed the festive frolics, and best of all getting up the Christmas deccies etc.

The hassle of struggling through the loft trying to find the boxes containing the tree, lights and the assortment of baubles, balls and balloons all disappears when finally they are all in place and the little twinkling lights sparkle off the glass of wine you are gripping fiercely in your sweaty hands.

"Ok, that's it, never again ..." you mutter, knowing fine well you will go through this same painful day every year for as long as you live. Someone once said, Christmas is just so special, they ought to have it every year ... Hmmmm.

The day starts well, probably a Saturday, and you are happily sipping a cuppa while thinking what quiet lazy activity you could fill the day with, something joyously exciting like downing a couple of pints with your friends while recalling some lurid details of recent happenings, sorting out most of the SIC Capital Programme and such like. Then … it happens … a voice calls out, *"When do you think you're going to get the Christmas tree down?"*

It's that sort of rhetorical question you have been dreading. Ho! Ho! Ho!

There is no excuse and secretly you actually want to get the deccies up and make the place look a bit more festive, as outside the day is horrible, a flying gale, driving rain, and the house needs brightening up. Elwood the cat, ever attentive, rolls over on his back, opens one eye and looks up at you … his mind turning over and you can see the smeeg spreading across his face, as he thinks … *"Oh, goody goody, boxes, baubles, tinsel, curses, mayhem … Fun, fun, fun!"*

Right, off we go, down with the roof ladder, up into the cold black world of the loft people, those invisible little beings who follow your every step in their world and cause you to do unimaginable things in contorted positions while using words not normally heard in happy domestic situations. Elwood takes up position at the foot of the ladder awaiting developments.

He doesn't have to wait long. When you're tall and crawling about on all fours on the rafters looking for boxes with a hand held torch it's only a matter of time before you bang your head on the exposed roof trusses. If only that was it, but inevitably that sets in motion a chain of events that leads to total disaster.

Yes I bang my head, but this makes me duck downwards at a speed far too fast for crawling, I then overshoot the next roof joist and so scrape my shin on the edge as my knee falls into the gap between the two floor joists. This unbalances me and I reach out to catch the following roof truss, which I miss by a mere fraction so am now in dive mode as my other leg follows the first into the gap between the joists. I drop the torch in an attempt to regain my balance and save myself but, too late, the second leg has disappeared into the fibreglass insulation and … oh yes, you've guessed it, through the plasterboard and into the downstairs bedroom. Marvellous.

Here we are, stuck with one leg swinging through the ceiling while the rest of me is spread across the rafters in considerable pain, as you can imagine, and a voice is heard to carry through the opening ... *"What are you doing up there, stop fooling about, you'll hurt yourself?"*

Fooling about ... I'll give you fooling about ...

"Ah ... Em ... I think I might need some help."

"What have you done now ... OH, MY GOD ... Is that your leg?"

"Well ... I don't think there's anybody else up here ..."

"For goodness sake ... Can I not trust you to do anything right ... Just a minute while I get the broom."

The broom ... ? *"What do you need a broom for?"*

"To push your leg back up again."

Hmmm ... ok, seems logical right enough. Elwood, meanwhile, is now sitting poised at the foot of the ladder, with an even bigger smile on his face, thinking ... *"Superb ... another classic start to the Christmas season ... How does he do it, every year a brand new trick ...? Brilliant."*

Some time later, with my leg retrieved, the ceiling plasterboard pushed back up and a master plan devised to repair same and floor the loft, we have found all the boxes and the rest and they are all now spread out on the sitting room floor. It's tree building time again. Whoopeee ...

This tree comes in sections and having labelled them all terribly well last year it will just be a doddle to construct this year. Firstly, the main upright section fits into the three-legged stand thingy with the screws attached and wobbly legs.

After a battle to get that together we get the upright bit in place then empty the branches out on the floor, six to each of the five levels. They are labelled D, F, G, H, I ... to correspond with the letters marked on the upright ... don't ask me what happened to E, possibly it could be too easily confused with F? So, we begin with 'I' on the bottom layer being the widest branches and work upwards, simple. In they go, each one snapping into place with the well oiled precision of a beautifully engineered piece of equipment that this tree is.

Onwards and upwards till we reach the final top section 'D' ... which I cannot find. Where is it? ... Then I hear a scruffly noise at the back of the settee. Elwood is on his back, section D held in all four feet as he wrestles like Big Daddy on the floor with it, chewing at the top pieces. On seeing me approaching he does a remarkable full turn and twist, leaps four feet in the air, shoots across the top of the settee and launches himself into the branches of the newly constructed tree.

For the love of God ... The whole thing sways back and fore violently and then starts to fall towards the TV. I make a lurch forward to catch the tree and nearly lose it all on the rug, but just catch the cat controlled missile before it lands on top of the television. Elwood hangs on in there then calmly steps off the tree, onto my head, down my back and neatly onto the floor, sits down, turns around and proceeds to clean his bum with his legs in the air. He'll have to go ... he really will.

On goes the top section D and we stand back and admire the finished article. Hmmmm ... All is not well with my tree. The bottom goes in and out like a yo-yo; there is something seriously wrong with the branches. Check and re-check, then finally it comes to light ... The bottom 'I' branches are in fact the 'H' branches. Ugh ... The whole blessed thing has to come apart again. Oh super. How did that happen? ... I and H ... turn it on its side and what does H look like? ... Well done ... a capital I. Next year it's numbers, definitely.

Another half an hour later and we have a tree, and what a beauty she is too. Cat-attacked branches, missing bits, bent bits, broken bits, lopsided, but she's bushy and bright green, so on with the deccies. Lights first though and ... Hah! ... new lights this year, no faffing around with old ones that never work, this is the real McCoy, just unwrap and wind around the tree, plug in and Hey Presto, it's *Jingle Bells* time again. Off we go, into the box and, of course, every strand, every bulb it seems is tied up with those twisted little black pieces of plastic wire.

You curse and swear as you think that you have got the last one out, then no, there's another little beggar, and then you finally get them all off and ...Boing! The whole thing explodes like a burst sofa, and all the coils of cable held tightly together by those pieces of wire find their freedom and leap out of the box in a huge mess all over the place. Another half an hour is spent unravelling the bloody things, and laying them out in a controlled line on the floor.

Great. Ok, let's get them on the tree. Start at the top and work downwards, winding them round and round in some sort of beautiful display arrangement. Half way down and everything comes to a standstill ... you tug on the cable, but no movement, in fact it seems to be going backwards ... Oh, for goodness sake. *"Elwood leave it! LEAVE IT! No ... NO!"* He runs away ... with the cable entangled in his rear leg, Oh God, the tree ... Elwood has more strength than Samson at this point as he assumes he is being 'captured' by some wild green tentacle, and as he shoots away the cable shortens up and BANG, over goes the tree, lights and all. I valiantly try to save all this and end up on the floor, tree on top and wrapped around with little bulbs. Minutes later I feel a cold but dry snuffling sensation in my ear ... it's him ... The Destroyer ... Get away you stupid cat, go and lie down. He'll have to go. Oh yes, no question at all.

It's back in place again, the lights are on, plugged in and looking good. White sparkly lights twinkle all around and now it's time to open the boxes and find those lovely little baubles and beads. Over the years we have accumulated loads of different decorations, which I guess shows how fashions and time change your perception of Christmas tree embellishment. Gone are the acres of tinsel, though they still are in the box, and lengths of coloured beads take their place; the round baubles are still there though, some going back many years and have memories all of their own.

On go the layers of beads, followed at the top of the tree by a spooky looking cross-eyed sparkly sheep in place of the usual angel, a couple of weird looking oversized chickens, some legless robins and then a myriad of coloured baubles in varying shapes and sizes. Elwood is in his element, this is 'party-time' ... Woo Hoo! ... He lies on the floor feigning lack of interest, but just waiting his moment of glory. I, meanwhile, keep a watchful eye on the little bugger, as I know of old that he will strike at anytime. Why don't I chuck him outside? Well,

Christmas just wouldn't be Christmas without this seasonal battle of wits, and secretly I enjoy it all, as otherwise it would just be a boring task with no ...

"Bloody hell, cat ...! Get out of there!" He's in the box already, quick as a flash. He was lying 'sleeping' a moment ago, head on his right paw tucked under his chin, eyes closed, stretched out on the rug, oblivious to all around him, and two seconds later he was in the box, wrapped up in tinsel, doing somersaults while juggling three balls in the air at the same time.

Oh, what the heck, just leave him. I line up the set of twelve peerie bright red balls on the floor, determining just where on the tree they should go, knowing full well that they will be moved later when I'm not around. My artistic talents are sadly lacking in the tree decoration front, and while I always think my selection and display is marvellous, somewhere in this house there hides the 'Tree Fairy' who quietly and over a period of days systematically moves all my decorations around and even removes and replaces some of them! I've never caught this apparition actually doing it, but I notice things have moved or disappeared day after day. I gave up asking years ago, but Elwood knows who it is. As usual he keeps shtum and just nods knowingly when I ask.

"Come here, Elwood!" ... No chance ... It's footy time. He's out of the box now with two big blue baubles and a length of green tinsel which has wrapped itself around his belly and he's playing keepy-uppy and dribbling the baubles all around the floor. Ronaldo doesn't have a look in; this cat would be worth millions in the Premier League ... if he could shoot. Have you ever played blow-push football with a cat? It's brilliant. He dribbles around my head while I lie stretched out on the floor and flick the balls back and fore at him, he in turn rises up on his back legs, dives down and flicks the baubles back with his paws, and hurtles round the room at breakneck speed ... Oh no, there go the cards! All over the floor, in among the baubles, the tinsel is still attached to him and a trailing length has now whipped past a second layer and brought them floating downwards. He's in his element now, two more circuits and a final Eddie the Eagle leap from

the window ledge on top of me and we wrestle back towards the settee. Magic. This is what Christmas is all about.

The ensuing noise and whoops of delight from both Elwood and me brings in the person who I suspect is the real 'Tree Fairy'. She looks at the scene of destruction in front of her and stands and shakes her head ... but with a great big smile and a giggle too. *"That cat will have to go, he just leads you astray ... Are we thinking we might have the tree up and decorated ...tonight, maybe?"*

No, there's nothing like Christmas for bringing out the child in all of us. With all the hassle that seems to go with the cards, presents, food, decorations etc., look past all that and play silly games with your partner, bairns, grand-bairns, cat, goldfish, whatever. You too can be really stupid, even if it's only for a moment ... Sure it helps if your cat or your husband is a few clowns short of a circus, but try it this year and have fun.

Cats or Dogs

Are you a cat person or a dog person? Apparently you cannot be both. The powers that be suggest that you are either one or the other, or possibly neither, hating the two species with equal venom.

I have to admit that I defy their logic as I am really probably both, having had a number of the beasts over a lifetime. We currently have a cat that we inherited and who has adopted us in a sense, but still remains the aloof, arrogant member of the feline species they all are. No amount of shows of affection by them will persuade me that cats actually care about you. It is all a ruse to ensure they will eventually rule the world. They are probably a bigger threat to world supremacy than Osama Bin Laden.

Dogs on the other hand are simple animals. Quite willing to run hour after hour chasing a ball and bringing it back to you to throw away again. They show huge amounts of love and drool affectionately over your shoes, trousers, face etc. They, however, cannot look after themselves, or at least not very well. They need us.

Cats, however, do not need us. They can and will survive on their own forever, long after we humans have failed to exist.

Some dogs have been bred to look like the backside of a bus, they cannot breathe properly, they cannot walk, and they cannot eat but sort of snuffle their food into a hole in their faces. Domestic cats, however, are virtually identical to all cats in the world. They walk, talk and move like a tiger or a lion. Have the same eyes and features of a leopard or a panther, and have a campaign to eliminate all humans. True, some have been bred to look hideous as well, but in the main they are virtually all the same. Whereas, if you look at dogs, where is the resemblance between, say, a Great Dane and a Chihuahua? No doubt the genetics are the same, but after that all similarity fails.

Dogs, however, are huge companions and will follow you everywhere, and no matter what you've done or said, will always be really pleased to see you. They are also a lot of fun and as I mentioned before, relatively simple, though some of them show an uncanny intelligence which is often harnessed for mans benefit. In my time we have had a Spaniel, a Shetland Sheepdog, a Jack Russell and half shares in other folks Labradors, Collies etc. The last dog we had was a great fellow. Max was a Jack Russell who grew up with my daughter and me. We thought the world of him though my wife, being more practical and sensible, realised very soon after we took him home that she was going to have a battle on her hands. Not that she didn't love him too, but was possibly less tolerant of his exploits than we were, having to clear up so much afterwards I imagine.

Like I said, he was a great wee dog, full of energy right up until he died aged 112, and a complete bampot. That's what makes dogs attractive I think, they have a huge personality, or at least some of them do. He generally was up for a laugh at all times. He had a cocky sort of temperament and liked to show off, and so chasing a ball and bringing it back turned into a dribbling match, and he could outshine any Premier League player in ball control. Possibly picking it up with his teeth and running wasn't meant to be part of it, and even with pumped up footballs he could puncture a hole in them in seconds if the desire was there.

Three-a-side was a great game. He generally was in goals and stood his ground, head cocked to the side, paws splayed out, muscles tight as a drum, occasionally checking your face but most times eyes glued to the ball awaiting its sudden kick from one of us. He never, ever missed a save, and even high balls caused no problem, leaping off the ground to head the ball clear before trapping it expertly on the ground. Sometimes loathe to slip it for the next penalty attempt he would casually let it roll away from him, only to dive on top again as soon as you made a move for it. Selfish hound.

Garden escape was often a problem as in his desire to meet friends and influence people he would leap over the wall onto the road and cause a near heart attack in some unsuspecting driver. This in turn led to a garden fence making project of huge proportions. At least this was my view. Some others in the household thought I was, as usual, making a meal of it. Either way, one Saturday morning a series of posts, boards, nails, hammers, shovels and such like were laid out on the lawn and a plan was drawn up for a barricade to keep Max in the back garden where he could roam around to his heart's delight. So, early in the day a series of holes were dug and posts driven in at various intervals, and the planking commenced. At times this was hindered by the sudden disappearance of the bag of nails. They were later seen travelling at high speed around the garden before systematically being shaken vigorously from side to side by a white projectile, which in turn ensured the nails in the bag were distributed all around the garden like bullet casings from a machine gun on full bore.

An hour or so later, having spent a considerable time picking up the nails with Max following me around in eager anticipation that this latest game would be available once more, it was back to the fence again. I got the planks all measured and marked up and eventually nailed them in situ. This was now the late afternoon and the little dog was patiently awaiting the final board being fixed, and viewed my handiwork with a rueful smile on his face. At last it was all in place and the back garden was securely separated from the front garden by a four foot high wooden fence, and the JR would be safely entrapped in the back garden.

I turned away, happy in the knowledge that a good day's work was completed and we need worry no more about stray dogs running around in the road, causing mayhem to the passing traffic, not forgetting the risk to his own life and limb. A couple of minutes later Max joined me tripping lightly beside my heels, as I wandered around inspecting the flower beds in the front garden. Max? How the Hell? I walked back to the fence and opened the gate and we both walked through. I stepped back quickly and closed the gate, as he nimbly leapt the four feet plus over the fence and landed smiling alongside me, stumpy tail wagging furiously, keen to show me his high jumping skills again. For the love of God! A whole day's work and he clears the fence with at least a foot to spare. What a waste of time. I eventually added extensions to the posts and harnessed two strands of wire to the top, which did deter him somewhat until he discovered that he could just clamber up the planks and slip under the wire. About half an hour later.

Car travel was not his favourite as this generally meant a visit to the Vets, and no dog or cat enjoys that little trip. However, on the odd occasion he accompanied me to the Rova Head or suchlike, it was spent in a frantic aerobic workout session where he dived around the back seat from left to right smearing the windows from top to bottom with his wet nose, climbed up on the back shelf and squashed his face against the rear screen and generally made faces at the drivers following. To add variety to this performance he used to turn round and waggle his backside at them. He eventually tired of this and instead launched himself directly from the back window onto my shoulder in a flying leap, scrabbling at the driver's seatback before tumbling headfirst onto my lap. I see now why they sell those dog restraints in those advertising booklets that fall out of the *Radio Times* or suchlike. I used to include them, along with the double slipper and the pole extension spider net-trap, on a score of 1 out of 10 in the items I desperately want to own. However, I may have to revise that rating.

In his latter years he became slightly incontinent, as sometimes happens to elderly men in their 90s, though it never hindered him in any way nor, to be honest, did it us, except that on a winter's night, in a howling gale and driving rain, getting him to go outside last thing at night was a nightmare. Standing outside while he persisted in attempting to go back inside without doing the necessary was a challenge to say the least. After an eternity, we both finally returned indoors, he shook himself and cheerfully trotted off to his food bowl while after some 30 minutes I had semi-dried my hair, my face, my shirt, my trousers and consigned my outerwear to the utility room to dry off sometime in the next 24 hours.

There was a spate of house visits at the time he dribbled loosely, by various sects of a religious leaning. I have nothing against these folks, they obviously have a mission to complete and while they were an occasional nuisance if the cup final was on or at an exciting point in a film, generally the conversation was short and sweet and they wandered off to try somebody else. This evening, the doorbell rang and Max and I answered the door to be confronted by those smart suited young men in full flow. I didn't have time to even say *"Hi"* before they launched into a long speil about the Seven Horsemen of the Apocalypse and so on. We both stood a bit perplexed as my several attempts to converse with them fell on stony ground. I was making no headway here, and didn't just want to close the door in their faces.

Max, however, had sized up the situation and wandered nonchalantly outside. He then slowly circled them and finally closed up on the one with the shiniest shoes and deftly lifted his leg, dribbling over the smart footwear. This did the trick, they all stopped in mid flow, looked fiercely down at Max, who in turn gave them his big-eyed soulful look and slowly lowered his leg and swaggered back into the house, turned round and eyed them both again. I in turn took quick advantage of the sudden silence and thanked them for calling, advised that we were not interested in their offering but wished them well on their travels and bade them goodnight. I then closed the door as Max turned on his heels and wandered back into the sitting room, where I swear I could see a large toothy grin spreading across his face. What a dog, I miss him.

Elwood, our inherited cat with attitude is another matter. He is a big softy at times and again I love him to bits, but he in turn, though affectionate enough, is no lifetime companion. He chooses the moments when he will turn on the leg weaving, the arched back manoeuvre, the heavy purring, the face to face encounters etc., knowing full well this will get him his dinner, his woolly mouse, his clearance to go rabbit hunting and so on. These are moments that come and go, and he decides when and where. Elsewhere you will have possibly read of his exploits and will have come to realise that Mr E is a serious basket case. I suppose in this we have a common link, but cats in general have a habit of doing some weird and wonderful things that are just an extension of their inner machinations.

These have all been listed elsewhere in a variety of mediums but the most common feline moves designed as a precursor to world domination are copied below together with a brief explanation.

Kneading – This comprises a session of slowly walking or just standing pushing down with their paws on your stomach. This often increases in intensity depending on the reaction. The second stage of this is the high jump attack whereby they leap onto the central belt area from an enormous height especially when you are just nodding off on the settee after a large meal. This can easily induce a cardiac arrest in the victim.

Spreading of Cat Litter – Those of you with town cats possibly find that this is a problem, as after doing the business, they systematically spread the stuff from pillar to post, only being satisfied when the tray is completely empty of all its contents. Outside cats on the other hand tend to bury their poo in a hole that could easily hide a large whale. These huge craters are then filled in by a serious digging manoeuvre that even Liebherr cannot compete with.

Staring – This is something all cats do very well and generally precludes an outright attack. It is quite scary if you are the intended victim, and consists of out-staring you while slowly closing the eyes into a slit, lowering the ears back prior to the quick swipe with the outstretched claws. Never ever take your eyes off them when they move into this position; it is fatal.

Delivering dead or semi-dead animals to you – This is a sign or possibly a warning that you may be next on their list. Sometimes the terminally injured bird or rabbit makes a remarkable recovery and goes charging round the house, garage, or shed etc., in an attempt to gain their freedom. At this point the cat almost always feigns interest and stares at you with a *"Well, it's your problem now pal,"* look.

Grass Eating – This is a pastime designed to cause a lot of problems later in the day or night. After having consumed copious amounts of long indigestible pieces of grass they crawl back into the house and find a quiet spot behind the settee or possibly just outside your bedroom door to spew up their last meal. This you generally find around 3am in the morning while on your way to the bathroom in the dark.

Sleeping on your PC – This sleeping is possibly ok if the machine is switched off, but walking straight across the keyboard as you frantically type in the last three digits of your credit card before the screen 'time-expires' is a No-No. I could live with that I guess, as it's hardly the end of the world, but why do they then turn and shove their bums in your face. Like I've said before, there's really no need for that.

Sprinting – This is the activity they indulge in when apparently startled that you have entered a room without their consent. They act as if completely spooked by your arrival, and wide-eyed shoot across the floor making deliberate attempts to cross directly in front of you. Not the shortest path to the exit I may add but often a circuitous route to ensure they trip you up while carrying three Tesco bags filled with meringues, eggs, bottles of wine, tomato sauce and an assortment of flaky biscuits and digestives.

If you have encountered any of these cunning little plans devised by the kings and queens of the domestic animal world, you have my sympathy. I have been there, got the t-shirt and the rest, however, I still wouldn't like to be without them. They enhance your life, make you more tolerant of others, cheer you up when you are down, and can at times be a real pain – but just like bairns and grandbairns they become a huge part of your life in the way a canary never, ever can.

Two Senior Moments

A Cautionary Tale

The other morning I drove up to Lerwick, relaxed and happy, listening to a new CD, immersed in the music and my own thoughts.

That 15-20 minute drive is a godsend for an old troubadour like me. I hum along safe in the knowledge that no other person can hear a thing and, at the same time, having driven the route many, many times before, I'm basically on autopilot and can assemble what little thoughts I have in some format other than the random mess they normally are first thing in the morning. The sun's shining, the day is bright, I'm singing a happy song and all is well.

I duly arrived at the car park, pretty near having sorted out most of what I needed to do that day, a collection of 'to do's' in my head in some semblance of order and a smile across my face as I had recalled a good day, great company and a few great fun moments from the 24 hours before. Everybody should have these 15 minutes of 'me' time, twice a day at least, where nothing interrupts you or your thoughts and you can dream for a moment or two.

I parked, locked up and trundled across to the main door of the supermarket.

Inside all was relatively quiet, it was early, but I couldn't see what I was looking for. I wandered the aisles, but no sign of my intended purchase was available.

I duly took up a stance behind the assorted folks at the 'quick checkout' counter to ask the assistant's help. The large woman in front of me checked out 23 items (I counted them out, and I counted them in), chatted, discussed their mutual friend Bertha's gammy leg, the cost of Fruit and Fibre cereal as against Shredded Wheat, online bingo, council back-pay and a few other world events I didn't just quite catch the theme of and finally said their goodbyes and she left. Next up was Gregory Nijinsky or some such foreigner from Eastern Europe, who wanted an unusually large assortment of scratch cards. He then took his time to stand and rub each one as he chose them and after what seemed an eternity eventually paid for them and gave them all back, having secured one win of meagre proportions.

At last it was my turn and while not unduly worried about the delays I was beginning to wane a little as my initial euphoria of a 'happy day' began to fade somewhat.

The peerie wife behind the counter is the usual early morning stalwart on duty there ... small, dark haired and resembling a Basset Hound puppy, with her hangdog expression which rarely moves.

"Hi," says I, with a smile. *"Is the 'Times' no in today, yet?"*

She stops, looks up and down the counter, looks at the rest of the folks behind me and then looks me straight in the eye and says ... *"It's Thursday ... "*

"Thursday? ... Thursday? ... Oh yea, so it is, sorry about that, got my days mixed up."

"Yea-aa ... it's Thursday," still looking at me with the Basset Hound profile, and I expected her to start slowly drooling at any moment.

I muttered something about not thinking right, and left. Her eyes followed me out of the building and then she looked at the rest of the queue and slowly shook her head and no doubt said something about stupid old men needing to be locked up. And rightly so.

So, there you go ... sometimes you can just become too relaxed, and please mind and come and visit me in Edward Thomason House, Cornhill, Kingseat or wherever they put me.

Oh, and bring a *Shetland Times* when you do ...

Moving Wall

I have this small peripheral vision problem which has both blighted and highlighted my life and career for many decades.

In the early days of 'coorting', on leaving the prospective in-laws house at Sandwick in the dark, and being the 'Toonie' that I was, my future wife would be standing alongside the old car in minutes while I arrived a while later, scratched and somewhat badly bruised, having blundered through Shetland Rose bushes, bounced off the harled walls of the byre, tripped and mangled myself in the barbed wire fences and eventually clawed my way along, hand over hand, to the side of the car. Mary, who can see for miles in the black dark, laughed nervously, shook her head and said ... *"What are you playing at ... for goodness sake get in the car and stop fooling around!"* Only later did she discover that this rambling about in the scenery was not deliberate, but entirely due to my lack of vision, and not eating enough carrots when I was younger.

Now, as time marches on and the twilight years beckon, there has been no improvement in the sight-seeing thing and once again I have suffered the slings and arrows of outrageous fortune.

That last cuppa before bed and a munch through a digestive is bliss ... but fatal. By two, three in the morning, the body has decided that no matter what the brain thinks, there is an accumulation of surplus fluid that needs to be emptied, and so I awake, lie there in the dark leaving the lights off so as not to awaken my sleeping partner, and then slowly sit up and swing my legs out over the bed. I can see bugger all, not a stymie, nothing. I rub my eyes ... still nothing. Oh well, there's nothing for it, I'll have to go. I rise slowly and pad as silently as I can through the bedroom, concentrating on the possible route through this all-enveloping darkness. So far so good, I manage to find the door and the handle and we venture forth into the passage. Now this is when it gets that little bit tricky, as by now I am completely disorientated and slow my forward pace to a mere shuffle as I try to visualise the position of the seat, the wall, and more importantly the opening opposite. Again luck is on my side and I clear those obstacles and a new found confidence ensues, as I increase my stride and pace towards the bathroom. Big mistake ...

Somehow, during the three hours or so that we have been asleep, some tosser has crept into the house and blatantly moved the wall between the hallway and the bathroom. How in the name of God we never heard them I'll never understand, but move it they have. As you do when you walk, one foot is leading the rest and boldly going forward, and so it was, as my left collection of neat little toes found the skirting of the partition in full stride, as my shoulder and head smacked into the uprights. Not wanting to disturb anyone, I stifled a scream and danced about in a style not unlike the Masi-Masi warriors and managed to stand in the cat's food bowls. This sent a shower of hard little tasty biscuits all over the floor, plus the bowl of water sprayed up and over me. Landing on the downward sequence of the 'WTFWT' section of the dance routine, I came down barefoot among the little 'Whiskas' treats and, while no one could see it, I'm sure my movements rivalled Michael Flatley's jumps in Riverdance. Jeez ... I had lost all feeling in my toes, my shoulder ached, and my head was spinning as I clattered into the wall and slid through the bathroom door. I managed at this point to switch on the bathroom light and burst into the room still partaking of the fervent Irish tap dancing programme.

Business completed I venture outside again into the black, dark world of the moveable walls. The bed-ward journey is equally harrowing as by now, having savoured the bright lights of the bathroom, I can see even less than before, which of course was nothing. This voyage is taken at a pace not akin to a snail, as I walk around with both my arms fully extended like a human Dalek, and after what seems a lifetime I finally collapse back into the bed, with a throbbing head, an aching shoulder and the middle toe on my left foot pulsating in time to some African beat. Just then I hear a muffled titter beside me ... *"What on earth wir you doing oot there?"* my wife enquires. *"Oh, you're awake then?"* says I. *"Awake?"* she says, *"I would think most of Levenwick will be awake noo ... it sounded like you and a herd of elephants wir having a party oot there."*

I'll give you party ... I recalled my desperate moment of pain and misfortune, which was met with more giggles, and the helpful opinion ... *"You should take a torch with you next time,"* as she turned over in the bed. Hmmmm ... If I ever find out who those midnight cowboys were who moved the wall last night, I'll have their guts for garters.

And do you know this, the cheeky beggars crept back in again after I finally fell asleep and moved the wall back, as when I arose in the morning, it was in the exact place it should have been. Would you credit it ... ?